MW00441914

Praise for Sam Wyly

"I cannot think of a proper way to salute Sam Wyly. He has accomplished a great deal, and his success has always been accomplished with honor and integrity."

—GEORGE H. W. BUSH

"I have known Sam for 50+ years. He's an American treasure. Texas and American business lore is replete with stories of entrepreneurs who hit big home runs in some industry, and usually done with much swagger. Sam's homers, at least seven that I can count, range across high tech, oil and gas, green energy, restaurants, retail and venture capital. More admirably, always done with humility, empathy and random acts of kindness. His children are walking commercials for his being a great father on top of all of this."

—ALAN STEELMAN
_Former Member of U.S. Congress (R–TX) and
Vice-Chairman Alexander Proudfoot Company_

"Sam led the board of directors of Michaels Stores. He made my position as CEO exciting. He had the vision and trust to let me run the company. I love Michaels today after 14 years of retirement. Our success would never have been possible without his influence and support. He definitely understood the balance between the board responsibilities and running the business. He was always very supportive of me and my team. He was fair, and always saw the bigger picture. Sam is certainly an amazing visionary, a successful entrepreneur and definitely lives the American dream."

—MICHAEL ROULEAU
Former CEO and President of Michaels Stores

"Anytime Sam writes a book, you should read it. You'll enjoy it, and you'll learn from it. This brief history of Sam's remarkable life illustrates his genius as a creator of pioneering companies and the positive effects he's had on so many lives along the way. An enjoyable way to get to know an extraordinary man."

—STERLING WILLIAMS
*Former CEO of Sterling Software
& Sterling Commerce Chairman of the Board*

"I put Sam on the short list of early pioneers who brought the Texas business swagger to the national stage. Today, businesses across the globe are looking to plant a flag in the Lone Star State."

—ED CURTIS JR.
*CEO and Founder of Y Texas, and Author of
"Why Texas: How Business Discovered the Lonestar State"*

"Sam Wyly's adventures in business span from computers to energy to even my love: restaurants. Every step of the way he is filled with a joyful engagement. Sam's journey reminds us that the American Dream is alive and well."

—KIMBAL MUSK
Founder and Owner of The Kitchen Restaurant Group

"Sam Wyly is an entrepreneurial genius who inspires both new business ideas and spiritual renewal."

—REV. CANON SALLY G. BINGHAM
Founder of The Regeneration Project

"Sam Wyly has been an extraordinary visionary for the long term."

—JOHN MACKEY
Founder of Whole Foods

"Sam Wyly is a wonderful American character: a natural entrepreneur and builder with an outsized personality and humor to match his success."

—WALTER ISAACSON
Former CEO of the Aspen Institute and
Author of "Einstein: His Life and Universe"

"Spanning four decades and remarkably diverse industries, the career of Sam Wyly—a true original—shows what good ideas, strong will and access to capital can accomplish."

—MICHAEL MILKEN
Former Chairman of The Milken Institute

Beyond Bubba

Beyond Bubba

The Life & Times of an Entrepreneur

Sam Wyly

with Laurie Matthews and Lisa Wyly

BROWN BOOKS
PUBLISHING GROUP

Beyond Bubba
The Life and Times of an Entrepreneur

Brown Books Publishing Group
Dallas, TX / New York, NY
www.BrownBooks.com
(972) 381-0009

A New Era in Publishing®

Publisher's Cataloging-In-Publication Data

Names: Wyly, Sam, author. | Matthews, Laurie (Laurie Louise), author. | Wyly, Lisa, author.
Title: Beyond Bubba : the life & times of an entrepreneur / Sam Wyly ; with Laurie Matthews and Lisa Wyly.
Description: Dallas, TX ; New York, NY : Brown Books Publishing Group, [2021] | Includes index.
Identifiers: ISBN 9781612545387
Subjects: LCSH: Wyly, Sam. | Businesspeople--United States--Biography. | Entrepreneurship--United States. | Billionaires--United States--Biography. | LCGFT: Autobiographies.
Classification: LCC HC102.5.W95 A3 2021 | DDC 338/.04092--dc23

ISBN 978-1-61254-538-7
LCCN 2021918803

Printed in the United States
10 9 8 7 6 5 4 3 2 1

For more information or to contact the author, please go to www.WylyBooks.com.

I DEDICATE THIS BOOK to my mama, Flora Evans Wyly, and my dad, Charles Joseph Wyly. Every Wednesday of every week (from the time I was in seventh grade and until I was a young man starting up University Computing Company), they wrote and distributed our hometown's newspaper, *The Delhi Dispatch*. And they did so without iPhones or any of the other handy computer-driven touchscreens of today. Their example taught me intellectual, spiritual, and physical discipline. After their newspaper days, I was very fortunate to have Mama and Daddy move to Dallas to live nearby, along with my brother Charles and Granddaddy Evans.

And a special thanks to my children—Evan, Laurie, Lisa, Kelly, Andrew, and Christiana—who managed my name change from Dad to "Papa Sam," after work had already changed it from Bubba to Sam.

The Bryn Mawr house where the twins were born
and where Sam lived when UCC was started.

FAMILY TRIP
Sam stands among some of his children, grandchildren, and great-grandchildren with Aspen Mountain in the background. All of Sam's six children have spouses, and three of his eighteen grandchildren have married. Sam has ten great-grandchildren.

300 Whiskey Yankee Gulfstream Jet on
company and family trips around the world.

Sterling, Sam, and Sam's brother, Charles (in background), at the Sterling
Software listing on the New York Stock Exchange. The company, and its
spin-off Sterling Commerce, were later sold for $8 billion.

Contents

From the Beginning and Beyond ...

1960s

UCC
University Computing Company served engineers, scientists and researchers

BONANZA
Grew to 600 steakhouses

1970s

EARTH RESOURCES
Oil refining and silver mining

DATRAN
US digital network to transmit data

1980s

STERLING SOFTWARE
Computer software and services

MICHAELS STORES
Grew to 1,250 arts and crafts stores

We wanted to be one of America's fastest growing companies, to be one of the best investments, and to be a good place to work."

—SAM WYLY, *American entrepreneur, businessman, author, and philanthropist*

2000s

RANGER CAPITAL
Small-cap stocks

GREEN MOUNTAIN ENERGY
Grew to be the largest retailer of cleaner electricity

EXPLORE BOOKSELLERS
Independent bookstore

1990s

MAVERICK CAPITAL
Hedge fund

STERLING COMMERCE
Electronic commerce software

Collaborating with Sam

"Any man can be a father, but it takes someone special to be a dad."

—ANNE GEDDES

WE'VE BEEN DOUBLY BLESSED by being twins. Sometimes we hear, "Here comes double trouble!" At the same time, there can be double the fun. We've also been doubly blessed by having two extraordinary parents. Our mother, unconditionally loving, smart, artistic, kind, and meek; and our father, an innovative serial entrepreneur who is eternally optimistic.

Our mother met our father when he was a newcomer to Dallas, Texas, in 1959. She may have caught a hint of his Bubba roots because at the Halloween dance where they met, he kept slipping out to his car to listen to the Ole Miss versus Louisiana State University football game on the radio. This game had the distinction of becoming the night of infamous Billy Cannon's run to win the game for the LSU Tigers. It was the fourth quarter, and this punt return ended up being the only touchdown scored.

FAMILY HOME
The Wyly family home on Beverly Drive, where Sam lived for fifty years.

By the time we were born, our father had already become a millionaire. The company that he had started had an initial public offering in 1965. By the time we were two years old, our dad had sold some of his company's stock to buy a big house for his growing family. We grew up in a town where our dad was pretty well-known, in a house that was like a mansion on Beverly Drive. We remember school friends commenting, "Your dad is Sam Wyly!" Although we had a sense of him being known, mostly life seemed like an episode of *Leave It to Beaver* (or *Beverly Hillbillies*, depending on which twin you ask) where the focus was more on our little idyllic world of childhood. We had family dinner most nights, and as we entered our teen years, we remember being regaled with stories at the dinner table.

Working on this book with Dad brought new meaning to the stories we heard growing up and inspired us to dig deeper into our family and American histories, since the American story is our story, too. While his stories are reflections on the lessons he learned, his experiences, and his takeaways, it has also provided an important insight for us. His discoveries are an inspiration for us to study the truth of that time, and the time leading up to it. While Dad's recollections are truly rosy—he rarely talks about his failures—he has taught us that failure is an important lesson in progress.

Lisa & Laurie

SHELTER IN PLACE
Sam's twin daughters Lisa and Laurie, leaving Royal Blue Grocery to bring Sam a latte.

DELHI HOUSE

Charles Jr. and Sam helped the contractor build the Delhi house as manual laborers at $0.75 an hour. The next summer, they worked as roustabouts on a natural gas pipeline for $1.30 an hour. They arrived at the jobsite on the back end of a truck, worked ten-hour days, six days a week, and still made it to church and Sunday school.

ROSIE THE RIVETER

Rosie represents the time period when Sam was growing up–the World War II years and afterward–when women entered the workforce, enabling 16 million to serve. This was a big part of the recovery effort in the United States.

Growing Up Bubba

"You're okay, Bubba! You are a perfect child of God."

— SAM'S MOM, *comforting him during childhood when he accidently pulled some iron cotton weights down upon his head*

OVER THE YEARS, I have witnessed again and again how family values and distinguishing qualities are passed down through the generations and how studying history is our best preparation for the future. Becoming an entrepreneur may have been an inevitability for me—lessons of entrepreneurship were woven into the very fiber of my childhood.

The first entrepreneurs I ever had known were my mama (Flora) and my daddy (Charles). I was born in 1934. After the Great Crash of 1929, times were tough. When I was a four-year-old boy, my parents had to sell their house in town and move to a clapboard cabin on Island Plantation in Lake Providence, Louisiana. The house in town had electricity, running water, indoor plumbing, lights, and a ceiling fan for the hot summer. The house on the island was lacking in all such

CLAPBOARD CABIN
A painting of a clapboard cabin very similar to the one Sam lived in from ages four to six.

BIRD'S EYE VIEW
An aerial photograph of Island Point, as the sun sets over Lake Providence.

modern conveniences. Just like the pioneers who settled America, we went outside to the hand pump to get water to drink, to cook, to bathe, and to go to the potty. Heat for cooking and warmth came from an iron stove that burned logs that we had chopped. It had been a rough few years for the cotton crop and hard times all over farm country in America. This meant we had to sell the house in town to pay down the crop loan at the bank. While this relocation was a wise move in terms of finances, it did not make getting to school very easy. Education was a value as important as entrepreneurship for my mom and dad, so while it was challenging to get to school, not attending was never an option.

One of my early memories is of a bitterly cold day in November of 1940. I was shivering, even in my

SAM'S FAMILY AT CAMP D
Sam (left) and his family stand outside of Camp D, where Flora was "Captain Wyly," captain of the women's prison at Angola.

WYLY BROTHERS
FloFlo, Sam's mother, with Charles Jr. and baby "Bubba" Sam (right).

warmest clothes, as my dad pulled hard on the oars of our boat to get me and my older brother Charles to school. (Charles was the one who bestowed me with the name "Bubba" when I was born.) There was a dirt road that was way too muddy to get our Ford truck through, so instead, we were transported to school by rowboat. My parents cared so deeply about education that if it meant we had to boat across Lake Providence and back each day to get me and my

FLORA IN HER PURPLE DRESS
A commissioned portrait of Sam's mom, Flora, at LSU, writing a letter to Sam's dad.

Flora was an avid reader and writer, a staunch supporter of the arts, and an accomplished dancer. She owned her own dance studio. Additionally, she was a talented seamstress who would barter slipcovers for food during the Depression. This is only a brief overview of the wide range of work Flora did throughout her lifetime, but being a mom to Sam and Charles was her biggest joy and what she considered to be her greatest accomplishment.

brother to first and second grade, respectively, so be it. Mama and Daddy always modeled perseverance and determination, traits integral to the success of an entrepreneur. Schooling, too, had always been a long-time family priority and privilege since well before my parents, and I see it still in the generations of Wylys who have come after me. The rowboat may have illustrated my parents' commitment to education, but we were not in that clapboard house for very long.

Only a couple of years later we would relocate to the Angola Prison in Louisiana, where my parents had gotten jobs. Mama was the first woman ever to be warden of the women's prison there, and Daddy

CHARLES J. WYLY SR.

A portrait of Sam's father by Evan Wilson, commissioned by Sam. This picture encapsulates many of the aspects of Sam's upbringing that helped to shape him. In the background is a sign for Western Union, one of the primary means of communication at that time. The typewriter speaks to their work in the newspaper industry, and the farm journal beside Charles is indicative of their land. Charles was always an avid reader, and behind him sits a stack of books, including *All the Kings Men* (the Huey Long story) and *Gone With The Wind*. Charles was a pivotal inspiration, who ignited within Sam a passion for entrepreneurship and education.

SUNDAY BEST
The Sewell brothers taking the Wyly boys for a wagon ride, all dressed in their Sunday clothes, including hats and suspenders, in the mid-1930s.

headed the pardons and paroles for both men and women. The prison was named Angola after the former plantation that occupied the piece of land. The Louisiana State Penitentiary was a maximum-security prison farm that many would call the "Alcatraz of the South." I attended third grade at Tunica School. It was outside the huge prison farm, and it had nine grades in three rooms. While at Angola, I learned a lot about the importance of redemption and second chances. I watched Mama do a great job at a position never before held by a woman, and I saw women were every bit as capable as men—although that wasn't necessarily the common perspective at the time. These were more lessons that would serve me well when I began building businesses later in life.

My parents saved their earnings from their work at Angola to buy a weekly newspaper in upstate Louisiana, *The Delhi Dispatch*. Daddy had always wanted to earn a living as a writer. He wrote the farming, business, sports, and political news for the paper. Mama did social and family reporting, in addition to running the telegraph agency and accounting and reports for their insurance company. She had "stringers" who got her local happenings in outlying communities like Epps, Mangham, Forest, and Monticello. We had a Monday midnight deadline for all news and the ads, which Daddy sold as well. The newspaper was printed on our second-hand offset press on Tuesdays and then sent to the post office for distribution. I made a trip with Daddy to East Texas to buy the press from a failed newspaper in a cotton gin town named Jonesboro. Mama and Daddy instilled a love of reading and writing in me. Newspaper work requires one to be resourceful, work well under pressure, and be able to uncover the truth, even in the most confusing or convoluted situations. Again, these were important lessons for me.

My parents' support of me and Charles never wavered, and that was particularly true once we got to Delhi High School. I would not say my place as a high school football player took up all my thoughts . . . but it took up a lot of them. High school football was practically a religion in our town. The goal at the start of every season was the same—to make it into the state playoffs. My junior year, when we finally beat Tallulah at the annual Thanksgiving Day Game, Mr.

OFFSET PRESS
Ken, the printer, and our offset press. At the time this was cutting technology and the *Delhi Dispatch* was the second newspaper in Louisiana to get an offset.

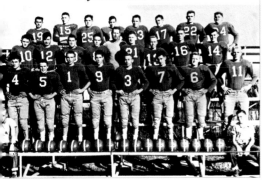

Delhi 1951 High
Class B State Champions
Raymond Richards · Coach

DELHI TEAM
This yearbook picture of Delhi 1951 Class B State Champions depicts Sam, No. 13, in the second row and Monroe, No. 17, in the third row. Sam's brother Charles is No. 3 in the first row.

Hugh King, a childhood best friend of my father who had become a US Mail Carrier, sent Dad a telegram: *"Le Rex Est Mort, Vive Le Roi!"* This translates to "The king is dead, long live the king!" which is a traditional proclamation made following the accession of a new monarch. After the Thanksgiving Day game, we won our first two playoff games, but lost the championship to Clinton High School near Baton Rouge, Louisiana. It was a long, sad ride home on a yellow school bus. We were determined, however, to win it all the next year, my senior year.

That year, being a boom town helped us out as the sons of roughnecks—highly skilled individuals who worked on the oil rigs handling specialized equipment and pressure controls—came to play on our team. Our two tackles, Jay Dupree, 220 pounds, and J. C. Duchene, 240, increased the average team weight I pulled down as a 155-pound nose guard, and we persuaded my older brother, Charles Jr., who had been due to graduate, to stay back another semester to help us win. The next year, we were state champs, and eight of the young men on our twenty-four-man team got athletic scholarships.

I had one teammate that year whose story stays with me to this day—that of my friend Monroe Fowler. He was a full-blooded Cherokee, and his parents had worked in the Oklahoma oil patch before they came to Louisiana, thanks to the oil discovery in the Delhi field. (Incidentally, that oil discovery brought our football team a lot of talent!) Monroe and I spent a lot of time together, and Monroe was poetic when he said that he could feel "the gentility of the Old South" when coming to dinner at Mama's house. College for

8 ⋮ BEYOND BUBBA

Monroe would not normally have been an option, were it not for some opportune circumstances in his favor. Working in the oil patch was often a generational expectation, and such was the case with Monroe. In those days, only a tiny percentage of students went to college. A high school education then would be equivalent to a college education today. Forgoing college was not seen as a good thing or a bad thing, but it was a normal thing. However, Monroe was a talented athlete, and he was destined for a different path.

My father was responsible for writing the sports section of the *Delhi Dispatch* and he would send it out to newspapers in the surrounding areas: *The Advocate of Baton Rouge*, *The New Orleans Picayune*, and *The Shreveport Times*, to name a few. As my dad wrote more and more about Monroe, more and more schools began to show interest in him, one of which was Louisiana Tech.

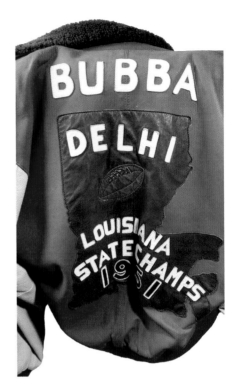

SAM'S LETTER JACKET
Sam's letterman jacket from 1951, the year his team won the state championship.

Suddenly, this young man, who had never envisioned a future that included higher education, had an opportunity he never could have dreamed of—attending college on a football scholarship! Multiple times Monroe expressed his gratitude to my family for helping to launch his career as an Air Force officer, but ultimately it was his talent, hard work, and determination to take advantage of this chance that resulted in his success. It was gratifying to see the doors that opened for Monroe. And thanks in part to him, my team won the State Championship!

Football and business have more in common than it may appear on the surface, and my football education taught me much of the persistence I would need

THE HITCHHIKER

AS MUCH AS I ENJOYED high school football, it was certainly not my only love—I also had a passion for history. I always felt the best way to prepare for the future was to study the past and use those lessons to shape our choices. One day while walking through the halls of Delhi High, I noticed a sign posted on the school bulletin board. It was a notice about an American History seminar at Northwestern State College in Natchitoches. It was a unique opportunity, and I knew I had to attend.

Attending, however, was not as easy as it seemed. For one thing, there was the obstacle of timing—going to this seminar would mean missing two full days of school. I approached my history teacher, Mr. Tom Judd, and expressed my burning desire to be present at this history seminar. I can only surmise that Mr. Judd was moved by my unusual aspiration to go to a two-day lecture, because not only did he give me permission to miss school Friday and Monday, he arranged to have my other teachers give their permission as well.

The next logistical challenge was that of geography and transportation; Natchitoches was more than 130 miles away, almost to Texas, and although I was sixteen years old and could drive, my parents needed our family car for work. So, I came to the only logical conclusion; I decided to hitch rides on the country roads that cobwebbed through the small towns in this stretch, which was mostly farmland, dotted by a few oil derricks along the way. Folks were friendly and had grown used to giving soldiers a ride toward home or back to their army base during the war. People in trucks or cars would stop and give me a ride as far as they were going in my direction, south and west of my hometown.

It took eight rides to get there, but I had left at daybreak and arrived just as it was getting dark. Most of the drivers I met loved to chat and would ask where I was going, and they would want to talk. They would say things such as, "I can take you about twenty-five miles and then you get rides on the road going west." I would ride as far as I could with each lift, and then I would hop out and begin searching for my next ride. I still recall one nice lady, who was heading to the market. She said, "Oh, you need the best road toward the college and it's only two miles out of my way, so I'll take you over!" It was a different time then, and while hitchhiking is not a mode of transport I would recommend in this day and age, I met a lot of kind people, I learned a lot, and I was able to attend my coveted American History seminar.

to call on again and again in my business endeavors. Stories such as my friend Monroe's also showed me the importance of looking past what could seem like limited opportunities.

The summer after I graduated high school, my father secured me a job as head page in the House of Representatives in Baton Rouge. During my time as a head page in the state legislature, I decided that after college, I wanted to be governor. My football team-mate Leamon Best convinced me that Louisiana Tech was the best place to prepare to run for governor (a position to which I was not even eligible to be elected until the age of thirty-six). So, off I went to college at Louisiana Tech, only seventy miles west of Delhi on Highway 80.

Once I arrived at Tech, I changed my major several times over the years, starting with Forestry (being a

SAM IN ROTC UNIFORM
Sam at boot camp in his
Air Force ROTC Uniform.

PSALM 23
A Psalm of David.

THE LORD *is* my shepherd;
I shall not want.

2 He maketh me to lie down
in green pastures: he leadeth
me beside the still waters.

3 He restoreth my soul: he
leadeth me in the paths of
righteousness for his name's
sake.

4 Yea, though I walk through
the valley of the shadow of
death, I will fear no evil: for
thou *art* with me; thy rod and
thy staff they comfort me.

5 Thou preparest a table
before me in the presence of
mine enemies: thou anointest
my head with oil; my cup
runneth over.

6 Surely goodness and mercy
shall follow me all the days of
my life: and I will dwell in the
house of the LORD for ever.

23RD PSALM
King James Version

Forest Ranger seemed like a good job) before finally finishing with an accounting major. I loved going to college. Dr. Ropp, the president of the school, spoke to all incoming freshmen at an assembly. He advised, "Tech is the friendliest college in the South. Speak to everyone you meet on campus." So, I tried to do just that. I introduced myself to everyone I met as Bubba Wyly and tried to learn the names of all my fellow students. In addition to enjoying the people I met at Tech, I loved the classes. English Literature and American History were two of my favorites.

I was also probably one of the few guys who actually enjoyed ROTC military drills. At that time, all American men had to register for military service at age eighteen. (In fact, fifty young men from Richland Parish were called for their exams the same month we won the High School State Championship; this was at the time of the Korean War.) My older uncles and cousins, back in their day, fulfilled their military obligation by fighting in World War II and the Korean War. At Louisiana Tech, all freshmen boys had a minimum of two years of Air Force ROTC. If we wanted to become officers, we were then required to commit to an additional two years of service. At Louisiana Tech I was Air Force #267067964 in Reserve Officer Training. (The USA became a volunteer-only military under President Nixon in 1973.)

When I was in my freshman year, fraternities were not allowed to recruit freshmen during their first semester, but I quickly observed that the Pikes (Pi Kappa Alpha) had some of the brightest scholars and best athletes of all the fraternities. When the Pikes came knocking on my door second semester, I learned that the main initiation was to recite the King James' version of Psalm 23, attributed to King David. This stood out to me because of the character and values that it represented. The Pikes told me that if I would join their fraternity, I could be the captain and coach of their touch football team (today called "flag football"). I had already noticed that the fastest sprinter and the fastest mile-long runner were Pikes—that would make an extremely competitive touch football team. I was sold! My dad had been a Pike at LSU, but what really influenced me to follow suit and join at Tech were the character and quality of the men.

THE GREAT DEBATERS
The movie poster from the 2007 film of *The Great Debaters*. This was the story of Wiley College's 1935 debate team, which won all but one of seventy-five debates, and beat Southern California. Sam's own college debate experience helped him understand and respect what a great job was done with the film. Sam has been a major financial donor to Wiley College. Also, Sam's friend Joe Kirven, who worked with Sam on Black capitalism, is an alumni and invited Sam to the premiere of the movie.

STUDENT PRESIDENT

While at Tech, I was elected by my classmates to the office of freshman class president, and later I became student senate president. I had campaign posters that said "Bubba Wyly for President!" My campaign manager was my friend Paul Hamrick from Shreveport, who went on to have a career in the Air Force. I considered this campaigning to be training for me as I worked toward my (then) goal of eventually becoming the governor of Louisiana.

Additionally, I joined debate team, which was both educational and enjoyable. We went to tournaments at other colleges where we argued alternately for and against a resolution. The topics of debate included "Red China" and free-trade—both still timely discussions today.

Another important choice I made in college was to take geology as my science credit. Geology gave me an understanding of the biggest economic impact industry around me at the time. It was studying the surface of the earth and rock structures underneath the earth. Oil was more likely to be found in sandstone—soft porous rock. So, I thought to myself, "It is not just all roughnecks and roustabouts, there is a science to the oil industry too!" College classes added to the knowledge I got from sending telegrams for Petroleum Engineers at our Western Union in Delhi and what I learned while working on a natural gas pipeline as a summer job. Geology as my science choice helped me later when founding a computing company serving oil and gas engineers for big companies and wildcatters.

All in all, college was an amazing experience. I was not there on the GI bill myself, but I witnessed firsthand how the GI Bill afforded many young men the opportunity to attend university. The GI Bill was one of the best acts ever passed by Congress, as it paid for the college education of all who served in our military after the Pearl Harbor attack on America. Some vets of the Korean War were at Louisiana Tech when I got there.

Dad had told me, "You get all the college you want, anywhere you want it—Harvard or Princeton or whatever, we will figure out how to pay for it." (But LSU and Tech were all I cared about. As my cousin Flo said, "Why would anyone want to live anywhere other than Lake Providence?" Those of us who grew up in Louisiana remember our "Cajun State" no matter where in the USA or the world we may later go.) My parents' commitment to education shaped me in a lot of ways during my childhood and continued to do so throughout my life.

I graduated Louisiana Tech with an offer from the University of Michigan to be their first Paton Scholar. After that summer, I drove my $1,500 1957 Chevy to Ann Arbor, Michigan, to earn my MBA. It was a great education at a wonderful and renowned school. How I got there, however, was an unlikely series of serendipities.

'55 CHEVY

DURING SAM'S LAST YEAR AT Louisiana Tech, his future was slightly uncertain, but most definitely promising. Sam had received a job offer from IBM, and as such was confident enough in his future steady paycheck to take out a loan to buy a blue and white '55 Chevy. After he accepted this position at IBM, his trajectory shifted, and Sam was offered the prestigious Paton Scholarship at University of Michigan. IBM said they would wait for him until he completed his MBA, but the issue of the bank loan needed to be addressed. As Sam often did, he sought counsel from his father, Charles Sr., who was a firm believer that a man's word was tied to his honor. He encouraged Sam to speak to the banker directly. Sam explained his situation. The banker told Sam, "Complete your MBA, finish boot camp, and when you start at IBM, then you can begin your payments." It was an example of trust and generosity that Sam never forgot.

UNIVERSITY OF MICHIGAN
SCHOOL OF BUSINESS ADMINISTRATION
ANN ARBOR

March 12, 1956

Mr. Evans Wyly
Box 332, Tech Station
Ruston, Louisiana

Dear Mr. Wyly:

Thanks for your letter and enclosed data sheet.

We are preparing a scholarship application form, intended especially for persons in accounting, and I hope to be able to send you a copy in a few days. In the meantime I'm asking the office to send you the regular forms required in applying for admission to the School of Business Administration, together with a copy of the School's latest announcement.

I feel that the prospect of awarding you a scholarship is good, although I'm not sure that the amount of the proposed grant will exceed the out-of-state tuition plus enough to cover books and incidentals.

Sincerely yours,

W. A. Paton

WAP:gf

*Enclosed

SAM'S SCHOLARSHIP
A letter from Dr. Paton at the School of Business Administration, discussing Sam's scholarship.

FIRST PATON SCHOLAR

William Andrew Paton was a great influence on the history of accounting education in this country. He received a PhD in economics in 1917 from the University of Michigan, and a scholarship was created by the school to commemorate his work. At some point during my senior year at Louisiana Tech, the renowned Dr. Paton came as a keynote speaker to our campus. As you can imagine, in rural Louisiana at that time, a man of his stature drew a huge crowd; we were a small school in a small town and not accustomed to frequent big-name visitors. Our school population was about 1,700, and our auditorium held about 700. Dr. Paton had a packed room, a full house. In fact, the audience Dr. Paton drew was equivalent to the crowd that came to see Hollywood actor William Bendix.

My accounting teacher, Mr. Harold J. Smolinski, had acted as Dr. Paton's host during the event. I was standing outside afterward as Dr. Paton and Mr. Smolinski walked out. At this point, I had not yet decided if, let alone where, I would be attending graduate school. I had already decided I would not be doing my military service as an officer, so I knew I had two years rather than four left ahead of me. Mr. Smolinski was well aware I was not sure as to what my next moves would be and that I had yet to even apply to graduate school.

In a smooth move that subsequently impacted the trajectory of my life, he said to Dr. Paton, "This is Sam Wyly; he is going to Harvard!" Realizing shrewdly that Dr. Paton's immediate reaction would be to interject and attempt to thwart this so-called plan of mine. As if on cue, Dr. Paton replied, "You can't go to

Harvard! Michigan has the best accounting school in the country—you need to go there!"

That was how I became the first Paton Scholar—via a lot of hard work; a crafty and wise professor; and a little bit of fortuity. It was quite an honor to be the first recipient. I studied both accounting and economics under Dr. Paton, and he was extremely skilled at simplifying even the most complex topics. The cold weather was a bit of a shock for someone Louisiana born and bred, but Ann Arbor and the education I received at The University of Michigan was well worth the threat of frostbite.

In addition to accounting, it was a treat learning about this new thing called a computer and how the engineers built it piece by piece. My education deepened on field trips with engineering professors to cities where we learned about how people were installing these monster new systems. Upon graduation, it was time to enter the workforce, and I could not wait to learn more. That may be one of the hallmarks of an entrepreneur: enjoy the work of the moment, but always be excited about what lies ahead!

• • •

Interestingly, as excited as I was about what was ahead of me, it seemed during my time at UofM that something was being left behind me as well—my nickname of Bubba. When I arrived at Michigan, although I was still introducing myself as Bubba, I was being called Sam. Evidently, there were not many Bubbas in the Midwest. It took a little getting used to, but accepting changes like childhood nicknames falling away is part of life. I was still Bubba on the inside.

WILLIAM ANDREW PATON
Professor of Accounting
Professor Emeritus
University of Michigan
1916-1959

Dr. Paton was one of the first theorists to argue that accounting should include the effects of inflation, changing replacement costs, fluctuating interest rates, and other economic factors in order to present a more accurate picture of a firm's fiscal position. In 1987, the American Institute of Certified Public Accountants named him Educator of the Century.

then ...

IT WAS OVER 360 YEARS AGO when my first Scottish ancestors, Katy Cleland and her family, braved a tough six-week-long sailboat trip over the Atlantic Ocean to be given fifty acres of farmland in America. They settled on Deer Creek, which flows into the Susquehanna River in Maryland, just south of the Amish settled land in Pennsylvania. My ancestors, and many like them, were "yeoman farmers"—those who owned their own modest farm and worked it primarily with family labor. They were the embodiment of the American ideals—virtuous, hardworking, independent. They cultivated the values upon which this country was built.

Education and entrepreneurship were tantamount family values for us. My mom's father, Granddaddy, was the town doctor. My dad's father was a lawyer. My dad attended LSU, and my mom attended Sophie Newcomb. Grandfather Wyly was first in his class at the University of Tennessee in 1876. Grandfather Wyly's dad was Samuel Y. Wyly, an 1836 grad of Princeton, who became a Presbyterian minister and educator in Tennessee.

My parents made it clear to me that no matter where I wanted to go for college and grad school, they would make it happen. They both came from educated families, although that did not mean there were not plenty of times they struggled. They embarked on several entrepreneurial endeavors that demonstrated the importance of calculated risks, perseverance, and fortitude. My parents were farmers who grew cotton, my mom opened her own dance studio, and together

CATHERINE CLELAND
A painting of Sam's Scottish ancestor, Katy Cleland, as she may have looked circa 1639. Sam commissioned this painting from David Wright.

PRINCETON GRAD

Sam stands with son Evan at his Princeton graduation in 1984.
Evan's son Mitchell is also a Princeton grad.

LISA IN BOSTON

Lisa in cap and gown, standing with Rosemary and Sam at her graduation with a master's degree in Deaf Education from Boston University.

they had an insurance company and a Western Union Franchise as well as a newspaper.

While home from college one year, I was looking over my dad's records, and I patiently advised him that since his insurance company was bringing in significantly more income than his newspaper, it would behoove him to sell the paper and focus more on insurance. Dad, in turn, smacked the table with his fist and said, "Bubba, you're a sophomore now, and this is the smartest you're ever going to be. I *like* that newspaper." It turned out Daddy was correct about this assessment as well; it's important to do what you love. The older I've grown the less answers I claim to have. That was another great lesson they taught me that I have tried to pass down to my kids—love what you do, and keep learning. Success is the quality of the journey.

SAM'S DAD AT LSU

Charles Joseph Wyly Sr. in the LSU yearbook, *The Gumbo*, 1926.

& now ...

BULLDOG BOOSTER HATS
Sam stands with his mother, father, and wife Rosemary at La Tech during the announcement of Sam's impending building dedication.

BECAUSE I, TOO, BELIEVE in educational opportunities, when I had the financial means, I dedicated buildings to various schools to help facilitate teaching and learning. One was the Wyly Tower of Learning at Louisiana Tech. Another was the Sam Wyly Hall at the University of Michigan. In Dallas, my brother Charles served on the advisory board of Alcuin School for years, and my daughter Laurie served on the board of trustees and also as president of the board. Early childhood education has been a focus of many of my children and their spouses. All of my children have some higher education.

My own parents' work at Angola so many years ago impacted even future generations' awareness of the importance of helping prisoners to be educated, thus reducing their chances of recidivism. Today my son Evan is on the board of a nonprofit called Maverick Capital Foundation that supports this and other educational causes. Several of my children and their children have found paths for themselves in the areas of both education and entrepreneurism. Today we can all be the yeoman farmer, the entrepreneur, the essential worker, and the one who works toward change and betterment, living out ideals upon which this country was built.

paying it forward

SAM WYLY HALL
The completed Sam Wyly Hall and sign outside at University of Michigan's Business School, above.

SAM WYLY HALL SKETCH
Sam stands with Dean Joe White looking over a sketch of the Sam Wyly Hall to be dedicated to the University of Michigan.

SAM WYLY HALL DEDICATION
Sam's wife, Cheryl (right), and daughter, Lisa (left), at the Sam Wyly Hall dedication.

WYLY TOWER
The completed Wyly Tower of Learning at Louisiana Tech University, named for Sam's dad, editor of *The Delhi Dispatch*. The sixteen-story tower is the tallest building between Shreveport, Louisiana, and Jackson, Mississippi.

WYLY TOWER DEDICATION
Lisa, Evan, and Laurie, all bundled up at the Wyly Tower of Learning dedication in April 1973.

A Defector from Team Goliath

The basic culture of IBM was that there were those of us who were fortunate enough to work for IBM, and then there were all the other unfortunate people in the world."

—SAM WYLY, *describing the corporate culture of his then employer IBM, back in the late '50s to early '60s*

BACK IN MY "BUBBA DAYS," IBM had come to Louisiana Tech my senior year to do interviews. This was not my first exposure to them; an IBM salesman had come to Delhi when I was in high school to help my dad at the newspaper office. He had come to sell us an electric typewriter. Even as a kid, I was impressed by how well this gentleman spoke, the confidence he exuded, and the Cadillac he drove. When IBM came to campus, the interviewers had the quintessential "good cop/bad cop" routine going. One man would tell me I probably didn't have a good chance at getting a job there, and the other would tell me what a great candidate I was to join them. Maybe they were just gauging how their prospective employees handled criticism and praise. Whatever their tactic was, it worked.

TEAM IBM
Front and center, Sam stands with his IBM team outside of their 4330 N. Central Expressway office building in 1959.

I wanted to join their company. I was thrilled to get an offer, but then things got complicated. I had also been granted the Paton Scholarship at the University of Michigan. It was a true dilemma—a good dilemma—but still a tough one. Upon learning of my scholarship offer and MBA opportunity, IBM encouraged me to get my grad degree and then work for them after I graduated. Things were falling into place; I got my MBA in 1957, I went through Air Force Boot Camp in San Antonio, and then I started working at IBM.

When I first got to IBM, they administered an aptitude test that indicated I was technologically minded. Because of those results, they tried to steer me toward analytic and design work. But I wanted to be a salesman, I knew it in my bones. And I knew I wanted to be in Dallas. Earlier, I had spent a summer in Dallas working for a family acquaintance. The work wasn't my most interesting job; it was with an auditing firm where most of my time was spent counting knives and forks in a tin building in the Trinity Industrial District—with no air-conditioning. And did I mention it was summer? Summer in Texas? Despite the suffocating heat, I liked the city a lot. I decided I wanted to work and live in Dallas. Except I wanted an air-conditioned apartment. (I call Willis Carrier the Patron Saint of Texas because he invented air conditioning—which must be at least as big a deal as Saint Patrick chasing the snakes out of Ireland.) IBM started me at the job I wanted, sales, with the territory I wanted, Dallas.

The IBM company culture basically taught us to believe we were the best and the brightest, working

Ross Perot and Sam Wyly
Management Course For Presidents
Upstate New York
July, 1965

SAM & ROSS PEROT

Sam attended a management course for presidents in 1965 and was surprised when he happened to run into his old friend and IBM "classmate" Ross Perot, who was also attending the seminar. Sam and Ross had both started their own companies in the early '60s and had both decided they needed a bit of guidance on how to be a company president.

for the best and the brightest. I was a devout believer. Not long after I started, however, a recession hit Texas. This recession meant I had to leave my position as a sales rep in Dallas and go to Fort Worth to be a machine operator. I was reluctant.

My boss told me, "You are going to need to move to Fort Worth."

I replied, "No. I like Dallas. I want to stay here!"

My boss then advised me, "There are four of you. Three will be let go. One will be moved to Fort Worth."

"You know what?" I said. "Fort Worth is sounding better all the time."

Like many things in life, this unexpected obstacle turned out to be a great opportunity. I was able to

UCC ZURICH
The Zurich office of UCC utilized IBM equipment; in the early 1970s, IBM data was stored via tape drives.

run jobs for IBM customers and really learn about their companies. One of the companies was a West Texas oil company; this education in oil would serve me very well later in life. At the time, though, I was getting to the other side of a recession.

Six months later, when the recession was over, I was able to get back to Dallas and get back to sales at IBM. Both IBM jobs laid great groundwork for my future as an entrepreneur because it was almost as if I was running my own small business in each position.

I was successful, and I was grateful, and after a while, I was also restless. I was twenty-six years old, and I had a wife and a young son, named Evan. We had a small house on a street called Marquette. It was a tiny house. One evening, we had my IBM training classmate Ross Perot and his wife Margot over for dinner. The space was tight and almost furniture-free, so we blocked one empty room off with a sheet. There may have been diapers drying

ROSS PEROT and I both had to learn how to be company presidents. Ross and I had a similar trajectory. He and I were both small-town guys. He grew up in Texarkana, just a few miles from my hometown of Delhi. He went to college at Texarkana Junior College for two years before entering the US Naval Academy at Annapolis, whereas I went to Louisiana Tech then into the Air Force. We were in the same IBM training class in Dallas, when we both had finished college and military duty. We both were true blue "IBMers" and felt it was the greatest company in the world. We both later left IBM and founded and built our own companies in different segments of the burgeoning computer revolution.

on a clothesline above us. It was not a good time to make a big change without a backup plan, but one thing an entrepreneur does is learn to listen to their gut.

There was an internal joke at IBM that the acronym for the company didn't stand for International Business Machines, but that IBM stood for "I've Been Moved." The company expected their power players, i.e., their 100% club, to get up and move, no questions asked, if they wanted to relocate you. I very much wanted to advance at IBM, but not as much as I wanted to stay in Dallas. Deep down I knew it was time to move on—even without a good backup plan in place. I made a decision to leave the company I had thought I would be at forever. I believed things would work out. I knew they would.

At that time in the computer market, there was IBM and then there was "the rest of them." It was time to look at the rest of them. People used to say it was IBM and the Seven Dwarfs. Honeywell was one of those dwarfs (although most people know them now for their thermostats). I was offered a job managing Honeywell's start-up, a mainframe computer business in Dallas. Being able to stay where I wanted and not have to relocate my family was a huge plus, on top of several other advantages. All of a sudden, I had a lot more territory, a lot more of a base salary, and a lot less cache behind my company's name. But I was responsible for building something, and that was exciting.

My territory covered two-and-a-half states—Oklahoma, Arkansas, and the northern half of Texas. My boss at Honeywell, who was up north in Chicago, spoke of Texas the way you might think someone would talk about Australia. He seemed to think I worked on the other side of the globe, not the other side of the country. He had a lot on his plate, and there was no room left for anything else. When I came on board, he told me, "Now Sam, if you have any problems . . . don't call me." He didn't have time for hand-holding, and that was just fine with me. In the two years he was my boss, I only spoke to him on the phone three or four times and I never once saw him face to face.

THE WYLYS IN BOSTON

I LIVED IN BOSTON for four months to be near the Honeywell headquarters in Wellesley Hills, Massachusetts. It was just off Route 128, which was where the minicomputers were born. My job with Honeywell began with learning how to write computer programs in their ARGUS programming language. There were others there that also had been recruited from IBM.

I rode The MTA (Boston's subway system), a railroad above ground but underground downtown where I stayed near Copley Square and Commonwealth Ave. Lisa and Evan also rode The MTA while living in Boston. Lisa attended Boston University, where she earned her master's degree in Deaf Education, and Evan attended Harvard Business School, where he earned his MBA.

The Kingston Trio, an American pop music group in the late '50s to late '60s, had a famous folk song titled "M.T.A." It was about a guy named Charlie who was destined to ride the MTA forever because of a fare increase. The lyrics included:

"Well, let me tell you of the story
of a man named Charlie
On a tragic and fateful day
He put ten cents in his pocket,
kissed his wife and family
Went to ride on the M-T-A . . .

Well, did he ever return?
No, he never returned
And his fate is still unlearned (what a pity)
He may ride forever
'neath the streets of Boston
He's the man who never returned . . ."

Statue of John Singleton Copley
in Boston's Copley Square.

I discovered I loved the autonomy of building my own team and managing them. I also learned something very valuable about managing people—if you have good employees, don't get in their way. This was a philosophy I would adhere to throughout the rest of my professional career.

I worked hard, I hired my team, and I went up against and took some deals from the Goliath that was IBM. My small sales team was outperforming several of the larger Honeywell offices, and I was making more money than I would have imagined. We had moved from our small house with its makeshift sheet wall into a two-story place on a lovely street in a great neighborhood. Some of the demons that plagued me at IBM revisited me at Honeywell. I did want to move up, but I did not want to relocate. I was not sure the two goals could co-exist in a big company. I did, however, have an idea that I felt would afford me the ability to stay in place, and afford Honeywell a great opportunity in an untapped market. I suggested to my higher-ups that they invest in a large-scale computer center in Dallas, one dedicated to serving the oil industry, military contractors, and other such customers. They didn't disagree with my vision, but they certainly didn't agree with it strongly enough to back me up. The Honeywell higher-ups didn't feel the cost-risk ratio made sense, and they declined to take me up on my idea.

• • •

I FOUND I was getting restless again. There was something else out there for me, and I was starting to suspect I was never going to find it working for someone else. It was time to try to branch out on my own and see if those business ideas I had been toying with truly had any merit. I thought, *How hard could it be?*

then ...

WHEN I STARTED AT IBM, I believed I would be a lifer; I thought I had arrived. What I didn't realize at the time was that there were so many procedures—and so much bureaucracy em-dash that new ideas were not welcomed but feared and argued against. It was not that IBM was not a great company, but innovation and trying new things is what propels us forward, and they were very committed to their "If it ain't broke, don't fix it" mentality. Even with additional freedom at Honeywell, the adversity to any risk thwarted us from moving further ahead.

What I learned at these two companies, however, was invaluable—and lessons I would use on a much bigger scale in the not-too-distant future when I was no longer challenging the leadership of one company, but rather, whole business monopolies. The other thing these experiences showed me was the importance of listening to my gut. Things are not always the way they seem, and the safe route isn't always the right route. I realized I had a propensity to disrupt the status quo—and that wasn't a bad thing at all. Although I left these jobs, I have huge respect for both companies. I am reminded of Honeywell when I adjust my thermostat, and I think of IBM when I see their Watson commercials as I watch football games. I am grateful I had the opportunity to work for both of these industry giants.

& now ...

THESE DAYS there is much less tolerance for industry domination and monopolistic practices. Innovation is embraced, but that doesn't mean it is always easy. When I was at IBM, I doubt many of their leaders would have envisioned a future where so many computer companies coexist, and technology thrives because of that shared vision among competitors. My disruption of company leadership graduated to disruption of whole industry monopolies, and that enabled changes that were and are better for consumers and society as a whole. I know now that when there is a nagging voice inside of us, we had best heed it and act! I had foreseen the need for outsourced computing services in the market, and when Honeywell refused to support that vision and put resources behind it, I struck out on my own.

Fine, I'll Do It Myself Then

I realized I was not likely to be made president of Honeywell. I was more likely to be fired for insubordination."

—SAM WYLY, *describing his decision to leave Honeywell at twenty-eight years old and branch out on his own to start University Computing Company*

IT WAS TIME TO BRING TO LIFE the concept I had been developing and then fostering while I was working at IBM then Honeywell. The Honeywell execs may not have seen the potential in my idea, but I had faith it was a good conceptualization. Technology in our industry was changing from electric machines to electronic machines, from hard-wired programs to stored programs. A new term, "computer software," had come into being. For years, I had been noticing the discrepancy between what the market needed, what the perception of the market was, and what the reality was. I was well-aware that a lot of people needed the power of a big computer system like I had been selling, but they didn't have the money to pay millions of dollars to obtain one. I saw an obvious gap: more people needed computer services than could afford them. I just needed to figure out how to fill that gap.

SAM AND MAYOR JONSSON
Sam with Dallas Mayor Erik Jonsson, sending a message to the Lord Mayor of London. Eric was a founder of Texas Instruments as well as a $50-a-year public servant, serving the City of Dallas.

SOUTHERN METHODIST UNIVERSITY
Dallas Hall on the SMU campus.

A new computer was $3 million, and there was no secondhand computer market then. However, there was a government contractor in Washington who had bought two computers, but the government said they were cutting the budget and needed to get rid of one of the two computers they had obtained. They were asking a mere $600,000. The next thing I needed was a loan. Turned out, asking for a $600,000 loan to float what you believe is a really great idea is a good way to make bankers laugh hard. I needed to elaborate on my plan. I had been talking to some engineers at Sun Oil and Texas Instruments, and it was clear they needed a mainframe.

As I had suggested to my higher-ups at Honeywell, people in the oil industry really needed access to this type of equipment. With potential customers in mind, next I needed a space for the massive system. Now, at the time, SMU could not afford a $3 million computer, but the trustees were willing to spend money on bricks and mortar. They could house the computer and pay for the electricity. I offered them a trade: if they housed it and paid for electricity—and this computer consumed a lot of electricity—the SMU professors and students could use the computer at night. (I was implementing bartering skills that I had learned from my mama during the Depression. Mama used to sew slip covers for couches that she would then swap with our neighbor Mrs. Vincini for pots of her spaghetti and meatballs.)

The single most important goal I had to achieve was securing a five-year contract from Sun Oil Company. Along with the contract, I needed insurance for the machine. A tiny company named New Hampshire

Insurance would sell me a bond that said, "If Sam doesn't pay, we will pay the $600,000 to the bank." I did not take a paycheck for a while. There was no payroll to begin with—I used SMU students for operators. With all these factors in place, I could secure a loan from First National Bank in Dallas for the $650,000 based on the Sun Oil contract and the bond. With that, my first company, University Computing Company, was born!

After just a couple of months, at the end of 1964, UCC had made over $65,000 in revenue, and expansion seemed imminent. After a brief spell when I was my only employee, it was time to once again build a team. I began hiring people for various aspects of the business. Some of the people I hired didn't make sense on paper, but they didn't need to make sense on paper. I followed my gut and chose those I would work with based on their talent and my intuition about what they could contribute. I knew what we needed to be successful. I learned when logic contradicted intuition that it was best to choose the latter. This was a good call on my part, and by 1964, UCC's first full year of revenue was almost $700,000. In September 1965, we decided to go public.

I think of September 1965 as a very good month in a very good year. On the ninth, public investors bought forty percent of our company for $1,000,000, and the price doubled on the first day. Two weeks earlier our underwriters, A.G. Edwards, headquartered in St. Louis, had said, "We have to cancel the deal; we can't sell the stock."

I replied, "We will take your name off the cover if you want, but we are going ahead." I could understand

UNIVERSITY COMPUTING COMPANY'S FIRST CUSTOMER
Sun Oil Co. Richardson Research Lab, circa 1960. Those familiar with Dallas will appreciate the lack of housing in Richardson at the time, and that the small two-lane road in front of the building is now North Central Expressway.

ROSS, SAM, AND BEN

Ross Rumore (at far left) was the first of what would eventually become 200,000 employees in jobs created by Sam Wyly companies. This picture was taken in Tulsa, Oklahoma, the first office opened outside of Dallas. The gentleman to the right of Sam is Ben Voth, UCC's first investor. Although Sam was not seeking out investors, Ben proactively offered to invest, recognizing that UCC would be one of the fastest-growing companies in America at that time. Sam had realized that his company would be expanding to other cities and, knowing this capital would be helpful, accepted Ben's offer to be a part.

their headquarters being fearful. Historically, Edwards had been brokers, not underwriters. This was their second underwriting ever, and they had a brand new, third-generation family ownership CEO, a nice guy named Ben. But a Dallas broker, Till Petrocci, with Eppler, Guerin, and Turner, was jumping up and down to have a stock offering for his investors.

UCC doubled in 1965. At this point, I gifted UCC stock to several of the friends and family who had helped me get to where I was, many of whom I had known so long they still referred to me as Bubba. I gave one hundred shares to various individuals, including high school and Sunday school teachers, some customers, my scout master, even my old "Big Blue" IBM training class friend, Ross Perot. (Then when Ross took his company, EDS, public a couple years later, he reciprocated by sending me some of his stock.) Our goal had been to grow UCC by

100 percent a year, and we did it! For five years in a row.

UCC's stock market value, after doubling in 1965, tripled in 1966, and was up seven-to-one (septupled), in 1967. In 1970, it was one of five companies headquartered in Texas with a market capitalization of $1 billion or more. The other great thing about September 1965? On the 22nd, my twin daughters Laurie and Lisa (the two co-authors of this book) were born!

Now that I was doing so well with computers, I had the opportunity to diversify. It was time to invest in other businesses. Most of those investments I made very intentionally. And one I made very accidentally. Another lesson of being an entrepreneur? Look at an accident as an opportunity in disguise. My next opportunity was to be disguised as a steakhouse.

EVAN AND TWINS
Four-year-old Evan stands next to his sisters, Laurie and Lisa, in their playpen at their Bryn Mawr house in 1965.

then ...

WHILE I WAS CONFIDENT in my idea, and as an entrepreneur I likely have a higher risk tolerance than most, I did not take the leap of faith I made when leaving Honeywell lightly. I was a young man with a wife and a two-year-old son to support. Additionally, the investment options available to entrepreneurs today—such as private equity and venture capital—were in far shorter supply back then, particularly for new ideas that weren't well understood by people outside of the technology industry. So, in addition to developing, selling, and operationalizing my concept, I had to build a business case to justify the investment that First National Bank and New Hampshire Insurance were making in it. This required selling the long-term strategic vision and associated upside, as well as the tactical nuts and bolts (going back to my high school football days—what we would call blocking and tackling) on how we would get there.

& now …

CLOUD COMPUTING, the concept I had envisioned at Honeywell and built at University Computing, is recognized today as the de facto standard for information technology. As hardware and software capabilities continued to advance from the mid-1960s forward, and particularly with the mass adoption of the Internet in the early '90s, the proliferation of data centers has powered the age of cloud computing in which the very ideas I had extolled—the ability to pay for processing power, storage, and software as a service—is seen in dominant platforms such as Microsoft Azure, Google Cloud, and Amazon Web Services (AWS). In fact, as of the writing of this book, Amazon Web services is the most significant financial contributor to Amazon, with their income comprising over 50 percent of the company's profit.

In early 2021, Jeff Bezos stepped down from his position as CEO of Amazon to be succeeded by the leader of Amazon's web services. These platforms have in turn led to significant innovation as software developers and businesses can now focus on improvements in their core products without having to invest as much in on-premise computing hardware and software (and the management thereof). My idea to leverage existing technology, and to create a new business model/customer delivery mechanism, then focus on specific customer business challenges (in our case—those of scientists and engineers in the oil and gas industry), can now be seen across virtually every vertical industry today. Companies like Salesforce (Customer Relationship Management or CRM); Workday (Human Capital Management or HCM); and Slack/Skype/Zoom/Webex (Communications) have fundamentally altered the ways in which businesses across the globe operate.

4

Congrats, Sam, You're the Proud New Owner of a Steakhouse

Once I thought it through, I went for it, whole hog. Because the best results come when you treat your ventures like missions. **"**

—SAM, *after discovering he was now the unintentional owner of a steakhouse called Bonanza*

BONANZA STEAKHOUSE was an accidental investment. (Accidental? *Yes. Accidental.*) In the late '60s, Mr. Gerald Mann, a gentleman I knew and had worked with, asked me for a favor; he had a company called Diversa, and he needed a guarantor on a note he had to their bankers. They were demanding immediate repayment of Gerald's loan. He was trying to sell a chain of steakhouses called Bonanza and was confident he could make a deal if he had six more months. But the only way for him to buy that time was for me to sign his note.

My mama had always said to me, "Never sign another man's note." It was good advice, which, this time, I ignored. You see, Gerald had

Bonanza International, Inc. 1977 Annual Report

BONANZA STEAKHOUSE
An image of one of the Bonanza restaurants that graced the cover of their 1977 Annual Report.

helped me get UCC launched through Diversa. He had helped me, and I wanted to help him. I realized there would be dire consequences for him if the bank foreclosed. There would be defaults and debts, and lots of people would be impacted. I knew PepsiCo had just acquired Frito-Lay, and they were looking to get into the restaurant business. Gerald and his brother Guy planned to sell Bonanza to Herman Lay of Frito-Lay. At this time, I had moved University Computing's HQ to the thirteenth floor of the Frito-Lay building. I knew Herman, I knew they were looking at restaurants, and I felt good this deal would go through. It didn't. Six months later, I was the proud new owner of a chain of steakhouse restaurants that I never wanted in the first place. (Not to mention I still had a computer business to run at this very same time.) But here I was! It was time to learn all about steakhouses. Even if I didn't know much about Bonanza the restaurant, at least I knew I liked the TV show it was named after.

Bonanza was the story of a ranching family. Their thousand-acre ranch was called the Ponderosa. Ben was the dad, and he had three sons: Adam, Hoss, and Little Joe. It took us a while to get the restaurant fixed up, but once we did, we decided to pay the stars of *Bonanza* to make appearances at grand openings. But before we had grand openings, we had a few not-so-grand closings to tend to.

I went to see Bonanza's chairman and president. I determined they didn't know what they were doing, and they needed to go. But I found a vice president, Jeff Rogers, who seemed smart and savvy and like he knew about the business—so I told him he was now in charge. We began visiting the restaurants together to figure out what was working and what was not. Bonanza had both franchises and company-owned stores. The franchises were doing far better, and I wanted to know why.

I learned that the franchises were run by families, and families seemed to do the best job. They took pride in their restaurant, they brought in people they trusted to help, and they always went the extra mile. Owning something incentivizes people to take care of it, to take pride in it, and to want to make it better. Over time we took the business from being partially franchised and partially company owned to totally franchised.

The company headquarters went from five thousand employees to fifty employees, acting as guides and resources for all the franchisees. Every year or two, we would have the Bonanza owners and their families to San Francisco or someplace like it, and we would work with them all morning, helping them think of ways to better their restaurant and bottom line. The afternoons and evenings were all theirs; they were able to enjoy the sights and sounds of the city. For the owner coming from Tupelo, Mississippi, for instance, San Fran was quite a great vacation. We provided the franchisee with information and education, and they chose what they wanted to take and implement and left what did not benefit them.

ALL THE FIXIN'S
Bonanza added a huge salad bar to the steak and potato dinner.

As I was learning about franchising steakhouses, I learned something else as well: owning the property on which the steakhouse sat could be even more burdensome than the restaurant itself. We had some poor-performing locations before I was able to take us to all franchises, and we owned those properties as well. So, even if we closed the place down, it was still expensive; we were still paying on a lease or land regardless of whether they were open or not. It was a valuable lesson about owning a chain, a lesson that would serve me quite well not too far down the road.

In the meantime, the '70s were a bad time to own anything, let alone a restaurant. Some factors of the period worked in our favor. Because times were tough, vacations and new cars and other big-ticket luxury items were unavailable to many, so small treats like going out to dinner became an accessible and reasonable indulgence for the family. Also, since many women were entering into the workforce, that traditional "housewife at home with an apron" idea started to shift. Oftentimes, Mom had worked all day, so if the family wanted to eat, they were going out to do it. But none of this offset the fact that during the painful '70s, the blue-collar sector was often the first to get hit with layoffs, and those hard-working people were our primary clientele.

I have always believed you find people to work for you who know what they are doing, and then you give them the autonomy to do it. Bonanza, like many others, was struggling. But I knew a guy who thrived on fixing struggling businesses (these are good people to know), so in 1974, I reached out to my "Mr. Fix It"–Don Thomson. He loved a challenge and

OUTSIDE SAM'S MALIBU HOME
Bonanza's Jeff Rogers and Ronnie Parker, sit with Evan, Don Thomson ("Mr. Fix It"), and Sam.

repairing a business. Once that business was fixed and flourishing, he got bored quickly and didn't have much interest in sticking around, but him leaving a flourishing business was definitely not my immediate concern. Don became Bonanza's new CEO. In a short time, about three years, he took us from being in the red to breaking even, to being in the black.

The Bonanzas continued to fare well, and it was good to know we had helped people with their livelihood and fed many families along the way. But I hadn't wanted Bonanza in the first place, and twenty years later, I was waiting for an opportunity to pass it along to someone else. Finally, that opportunity presented itself in the form of John Kluge, a billionaire who had made his money in cell phones. Now Kluge, surprisingly at least to me, wanted to break into the steakhouse market. When I asked him why, he said he used to drive a Frito-Lay truck and sell to these guys. I had owned the restaurant for over twenty years and through three recessions. I didn't want to own it through another. I sold to John and said goodbye to my restaurant days. Or so I thought.

· · ·

DURING THE BONANZA DAYS, I was very into the Pritikin Principle, a low-fat diet based on veggies, grains, fruits, fish, and lean protein. It is a healthy and earth-based way of eating and part of the reason we installed salad bars in all the Bonanzas. I wanted to offer more nutritional and healthy options. (Some people were surprised by how well received the salad bars were, but I was not. Turns out even cowboys want some good green stuff on their plate.) Many years later, in 2007, I purchased a bookstore. But it wasn't just a bookstore; there was a bistro in the attic. The plant-based, planet-friendly type of eating I had advocated for years before was the type of food you could find in this Aspen-based bookstore/bistro I had bought.

then ...

I COME FROM A LONG LINE OF FARMERS; my family worked the land for many generations. When Doc Evans, my granddaddy, was practicing medicine, he would exalt the virtues of the sweet potato, among other healthy foods. There is always a certain amount of trend following when it comes to food, but even back in the '70s, when many considered TV dinners the ultimate meal and some thought of mac 'n cheese as a vegetable, my connection to the farmers in my family always had me craving food that came straight from the earth, like fruits and veggies. The salad bars at the Bonanzas were one way I could accomplish that. This is not to say I was always the model of clean eating. I'm still a southern boy and have had more than my fair share of fried foods along the way. My favorite restaurant growing up (in a time when there were generally only a couple restaurants around) was called *Saljobar,* named for the owner's daughters Sally,

Joleen, and Barbara. It was more of a gathering place, and to this day I have fond memories of being there and running into friends and neighbors. Restaurants can be places that feed our souls as well as our stomachs, and that was part of what made Bonanza an interesting undertaking for me—it wasn't just about the food, it was also about the families coming in to break bread together, as well as

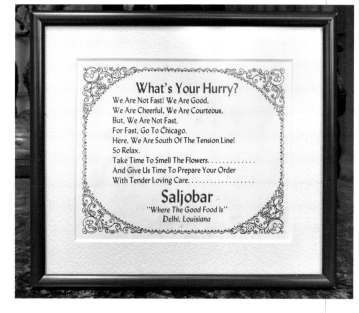

the families that owned the franchises. Interestingly, I wasn't the only member of my family who embraced the concept of healthy eating, and, more specifically, at least eventually, healthy restaurants.

FARMERS IN THE FAMILY!
Sam's daughter Christiana stands with her husband Kimbal Musk at one of their family restaurants. Christiana is wearing Sam's FFA (Future Farmers of America) jacket from his high school days back in Delhi.

& now ...

THESE DAYS we still have a few farmers in the family. It is interesting to see how much more we know now than we used to about the environmental impact our food choices have on our planet. When my family came over to this country over 360 years ago, living off the land was the only option, and it was done primarily via our hands and our tools, so intrinsically, it was done in an environmentally friendly way. Over the years, efficiency and mass production of everything from cotton to cattle had some ramifications that we now have to work to correct. Christiana has made it part of her life's mission to do so. Christiana did research at City University of London, that focused on the future of meat from a food policy perspective. Food policy is a relatively new concept that deals specifically with how food is made, distributed, purchased, or dispensed and how that impacts the planet, agriculture, and human health needs. She has worked to help develop critical research on the livestock and climate change and the importance of sustainable diets.

The other commonality Christiana and I now share is that of restaurant ownership. Christiana and her husband, Kimbal Musk, have a Boulder-based restaurant with locations across the country. Their focus is to create healthy food, available at all price points, and sourced from American farmers. These restaurants, The Kitchen American Bistro, Next Door, and Hedge Row, employ hundreds of people and donates back to Christiana and Kimbal's nonprofit, Big Green, which is a nationwide network of learning gardens and food literacy programs. This is a concept built around the idea that having the skills and knowledge to grow and prepare healthy food can help shift the issues so many individuals face in terms of health challenges, simply because they lack the information and/or access to make optimal dietary choices. The salad bars at Bonanza way back when were a great start and one I am proud of, but seeing the changes happening on both a societal and global scale in reference to our relationship with food is an inspiring shift and one we are all fortunate to be witnessing.

SAM, NIXON, AND JOE

"Mr. President, this is Joe Kirven, president of the Dallas Negro Chamber of Commerce."
Nixon made a campaign promise to promote Black capitalism (setting up loans and
other aid for blacks to start their own businesses). Sam was appointed chairman of the
president's Advisory Commission on Minority Enterprises, and Joe Kirven was a member.

5

What Goes Up Must Come Down

I sensed that there was potential trouble coming for paper assets like stocks and bonds and looked at hard assets like oil, gold, silver, and real estate."

—SAM WYLY, *describing why he felt it was time to diversify even while UCC was flourishing*

IN THE LATE '60S, around the same time I made my accidental investment in Bonanza, I made a deliberate investment. UCC had been growing fast, it was valued highly, and it was time to diversify our assets. We needed to have some assets that would benefit from inflation, although I had no way to know just how bad inflation was soon going to get. Oil was part of my life from when I was a kid growing up in the oil fields of Louisiana. I knew the roughnecks and their kids. I had also done work with oilmen while at IBM, Honeywell, and UCC. Back in Lake Providence, my cousin Opp Guenard had an ESSO truck to take fuel to farmers and gas stations. My childhood was spent in the oil patch surrounding our *Delhi Dispatch* newspaper and I was

COUSIN OPP'S ESSO TRUCK
Sam's cousin, Opp Guenard, and his ESSO truck in which he delivered fuel to farmers and gas stations around Lake Providence.

enchanted by the massive ESSO Baton Rouge Refinery. So presently, in my business, I was wondering how to wisely get deeper into hard assets such as oil, gold, and silver.

My Dallas bankers said Mr. Eugene Constantine wanted to sell his Memphis refinery, the perfect little oil refinery on the banks of the Mississippi. It wasn't the monster that the Baton Rouge Refinery was, but at the same time we bought it, we bought a different company that had a team of geologists, as well as exploration prospects in copper, silver, and uranium. It was called Vitro, located in Golden, Colorado, next door to the Colorado School of Mines. We combined the two entities and launched a company we called Earth Resources. We hired a man named Dan Krause, whom I knew from the Young Presidents Organization, as our Chief Executive Officer.

FAIRBANKS, ALASKA, 1979
Construction of Earth Resources' Alaskan refinery.

Earth Resources was a great twelve-year run for us. The Memphis refinery revenue grew hugely—and surprisingly—because of Fred Smith. Fred was a Memphis native and Yale graduate who had had an idea for overnight mail/package delivery to or from any metro area in the country. The way this worked was by having packages routed to a central hub in Memphis every night, and then shipped back out to the delivery destinations the following morning. He called his company Federal Express. They bought a lot of jet fuel—a huge boon for our Memphis refinery. And it was our team of Memphis refinery managers who gave me the confidence to build a grassroots refinery in Fairbanks, Alaska, after the large oil discovery on the North Slope. A super pipeline was being laid to

FEDERAL EXPRESS
A fleet of Federal Express Airplanes, circa 1970. FedEx was the biggest customer of the Memphis Refinery and a significant part of the reason the refinery needed to expand.

DeLAMAR SILVER MINE
An image of the Earth Resources Company logo, etched into a bar of silver. The silver ore was produced in the DeLamar Silver Mine on the boarder of Idaho and Oregon.

carry crude oil down to Valdez, which would then be carried by oil tankers down to Long Beach, California. Our biggest customers were airlines who flew over the North Pole to Japan, China, and Korea.

In 1981, Dallas's economic fortunes slid into precipitous decline, as "busts" in the city's three booming industries at the time—oil, real estate, and banking—combined to wreak havoc on the regional economy. In 1986, the price in oil declined to $11 a barrel (bbl), after having been at nearly $40/bbl at the beginning of the decade. Adjusted for inflation, this would be the equivalent in 2020 dollars of a reduction from $110/bbl to $26/bbl. Ninety percent of Dallas's oil and real estate millionaires found themselves "busted." Compounding this, a savings and loan crisis led to the failure of nine of the ten largest banks in Texas. Many lost jobs, and unemployment soared. The same story was happening all over the country.

My family was fortunate to see it coming as the prices of silver and gold and other "hard" assets were soaring in the inflationary 1970s. We had the DeLamar Silver Mine in Idaho, developed by our Golden, Colorado guys, along with oil refineries in Memphis and in Fairbanks, all in our Earth Resources company—which we sold in 1980. The price of silver today is less than what it was in the 1970s. In order to sell the company, we had to oppose our CEO and other directors who had a consultant's report that said everything was going to continue along the same financially successful trajectory. It was rumored that fellow Dallasites, the Hunt brothers, along with Saudi Arabians, were buying up all the silver bullion and futures on the market. So, I asked them if they would like to buy our silver mine—and they did. But our CEO, Dan Krause, opposed the sale, and he persuaded a majority (four of seven) of the board to support his point of view. In response, I worked to sway the other owners of the company to throw out opposing directors so we could sell the company. I knew a crash in inflation-based assets was coming, but they just did not get it. Fellow director Jimmy Perkins, who had merged his family's Tennessee gas stations into Earth Resources, joined us in the proxy fight. Jimmy could think like an owner, like us.

I am naturally a peaceful sort, not a pugilist, but I had learned to fight for what was right. I embarked on a proxy fight to replace that board group. Our family owned 20 percent of the company, and the Perkins, 5 percent, so Dan knew he was likely to lose the proxy fight. He also started marketing the company to potential buyers. Thankfully, we were able to sell just before the big crash hit, and at a 40 percent premium to the prior market price. Big institutions in that day almost always backed the CEO and board majority in a proxy fight. But not this time.

The buyer was Mapco out of Tulsa. The refinery is a lot bigger today with more jobs. Their pipeline company fit with the refinery.

then ...

WHEN WE STARTED EARTH RESOURCES, silver and oil were at bargain basement prices. Silver was $2 an ounce and oil was going for less than $3/bbl. Nixon took the US off the gold standard and put price controls in place. Then the Israeli-Egyptian War (also known as the Yom Kippur War or the Fourth Arab-Israeli War) broke out in 1973, and the US sided with Israel, so then there was a retaliatory Arab oil embargo. Prices shot up from $3/bbl to $12/bbl and all of a sudden people were standing in line for hours at the gas pump. I realized there was a big gap between what Earth Resources was being traded at and the value of its assets. It was also clear to me the oil scarcity was going to implode and prices would come crashing down. In other words, a lot of people were seeing what they wanted to see about the economic future, and not what my gut was telling me was looming around the corner.

& now ...

AS I HAVE WRITTEN THIS BOOK during the global COVID-19 pandemic, the combined pressures of plummeting demand for oil and gas and the glut in global supply levels have pushed prices to ten-year lows.

On April 20, 2020, the price of oil went negative for the first time in trading history. There wasn't enough storage capacity to absorb the excess supply. Add the increasing societal pressures (and consumer preferences) for more sustainable energy production and business practices, perhaps the best hard assets of the twenty-first century will no longer be oil, gas, silver, and gold, but the materials that go into wind turbines and solar panels, and the lithium used to make batteries for electric vehicles and the electric grid.

It Was Written in the Stars

"Not all my business endeavors were successes, and there were certainly tough years along the way."

—SAM WYLY

THE LATE '60S AND THE '70S were a really tough time. American unity behind our "hold the line" policy toward the Russian and Chinese Communists was falling apart with our cost in blood in Vietnam. The country spent heavily on its Cold War arms race with the Soviet Union and the hot war against Communist expansion in Vietnam, as well as President Johnson's Great Society programs at home. The defining, and in many ways most excruciating, year for the nation in those times was 1968. Robert Kennedy and Martin Luther King Jr. were murdered, and our inner cities burned. Somebody actually invented an economic misery index by adding unemployment to the inflation rate and coming up with a number to quantify the pain being felt by the average American. Other than the Great Depression years of the 1930s, no decade of the twentieth century had a misery

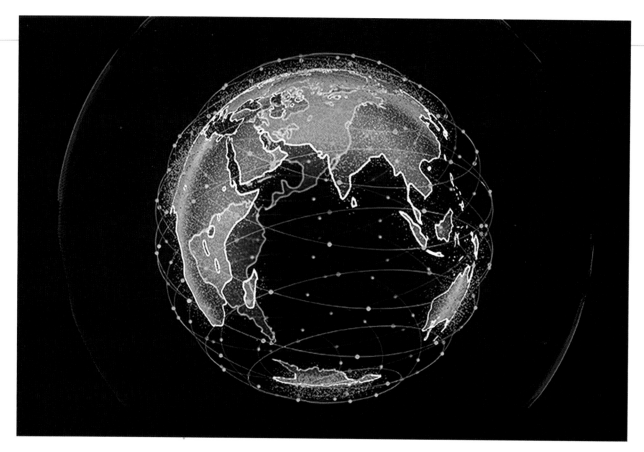

STARLINK
A graphic rendering of the earth ensconced in the unified satellite system.
Eventually, this will be the means by which internet is available to all and
a greater connection to our fellow human beings is established.

Beginning in the 1960s, my father Sam helped build the telecommunications foundation for what became the internet. He and his brother Charles led the wave from computer hardware to software and enabled the creation of communication superhighways by breaking down the monopolies that prevented innovation. My husband, Kimbal Musk, and his brother, Elon Musk, picked up where they left off, helping build the first generation of the internet. Both sets of brothers sold their internet companies in 1999, the year that I graduated from high school—just before the great crash of the .com boom."

—CHRISTIANA WYLY MUSK, *describing the*
evolution of her dad's satellite concept

BERNIE STRASSBURG, FCC

Sam and Ray Cotton (a Datran head of marketing) stand with Bernie Strassburg (left), head of the Federal Communications Commission (FCC), as they discuss disassembling the phone company monopolies. It was greatly helpful and significant to have Bernie and the FCC on Sam's side.

index as painful as that of the 1970s. The country had paid dearly for Lyndon Johnson's guns and butter policy, simultaneously paying for both social welfare programs and war.

It was during this tumultuous time I embarked on a mission to alter the trajectory of computers and communication. I knew that there was untapped potential in the world of computers, but I also knew it would not be accessible until computers could talk to each other quickly, efficiently, and inexpensively. I comprised a team of brilliant minds who I knew could help me see this vision to fruition. My team included Sy Joffe,

UCC DATRAN
Women working at the
London Data Center, 1968.

who was a bright and accomplished telecommuni-cations engineer from UNIVAC (Universal Automatic Computer, the first general-purpose electronic digital computer). He shared my belief that computers were destined to become the primary means of commu-nication. We wanted to build a digital network, an information superhighway, and we named our com-pany Data Transmission Company—or Datran.

Our plan/goal was to build digital radio transmit-ters across the country, about twenty miles apart from each other. There was a hefty obstacle, though, in the form of a big business monopoly—AT&T. They were absolutely not wishing for our success. I headquartered Datran in DC because I knew we needed to be visible there, and I knew the Federal Communications Commission (FCC) needed to be very aware of who we were and that we would not be bullied. At least that was the goal.

All the advice I was getting (and I was getting *a lot* of advice) was about how tough it was to compete with "Ma Bell" and how nobody could beat the phone monopoly. There was only one permanent seat on the biggest bank board—and that seat was the telephone monopoly's seat. This same story held true in every city.

The telephone monopoly was able to slow the process of our development to an almost debilitating pace. And why wouldn't they want to thwart us? We planned to offer a better quality, faster, less expensive alternative to what they were doing. We irrefutably proved there was a demand for a separate digital network, and after we proved that AT&T tried a different tack to usurp us: claiming monopoly status assures the best service.

It took five years . . . five long, expensive, and exhausting years. Although the FCC did not have the power to disassemble AT&T, they were able to mandate that competition in data transmission was, as I had believed, the best thing for consumers.

AT&T bullied and badgered those who wanted to work with us. The Bell monopoly ruthlessly exploited their power in Congress by trying to pass the Bell Bill, which would override the FCC's recommended policy for competitive markets. This was a bill authored by a *third* of Congress and when introduced would have given Bell complete and total control of all data

UCC WORLDWIDE SERVICES
A depiction of the way UCC's digital services were forced to travel over analog lines; this transmission of data was more cumbersome, more expensive, and bits of data often got lost along the way.

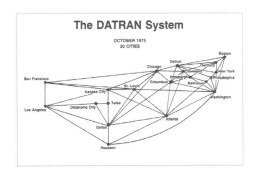

THE DATRAN SYSTEM
Sam wanted to build a highway for computers, and this was the map of the planned Datran Network.

communications on top of all the voice communications that they already owned. This brazen move was a strong indication of how things that were already tough and would continue to be tough. The fact that one-third of Congress introduced the bill was an indicator of the political power of the telephone monopoly. The bill did not get passed, but a free market was still a ways away.

We had built part of the network we envisioned, between Houston and Chicago. When we activated the fifty-nine microwave towers that connected the cities with each other, everything worked! We had proved ourselves. But then AT&T entered our market with a data service, they raised prices on local and long-distance phone calls, and undercut our price by 40 percent.

In August 1976, after spending eight long years and $100 million, I shut down Datran and had to let go of three hundred of the best and brightest telecommunications engineers in America. Although the company was now defunct, I knew on principle to protect consumers and consumerism. This was not a fight I could walk away from. I dragged AT&T into court with an anti-monopoly suit. It is worth noting I am not a litigious person. Earlier, multiple possible lawsuits were presented to me over the years against my former employer, IBM. I was not interested in these because I was not about to sue someone for gratuitous reasons. In this instance, there was a very valid reason to file suit. When filing a monopoly lawsuit, one must ask themselves two questions: Does a company have monopoly power? And, does that monopoly abuse their power?

In the other cases, such as with IBM, they had monopoly power, but I did not believe there was evidence of abuse. In this instance, however, there most assuredly was evidence of AT&T's abuse. After years of battle, AT&T settled. UCC recovered $50 million and ended AT&T's monopoly power in 1982.

Our antitrust lawsuit, which was joined by the FCC, is what busted up the telephone monopoly into eight different pieces. What was previously one massive monopoly transitioned into eight different companies competing with each other, and this is what really generated good competition: bringing the cost down and the quality up, and facilitating the innovation that helped create the internet and that made computers more accessible for all.

then ...

BY 1966, I KNEW there were infinite possibilities for computers to launch us into the future we all envisioned. A future previously only imagined, our fantasies tickled by science fiction books and movies, was now something we would see fleeting glimpses of in the realms of reality. Sputnik 1, the first artificial earth satellite, was launched by the Soviet Union in October 1957. Cold War implications aside, this was a pivotal moment for technology.

It was clear to me that until computers could communicate with each other quickly and easily, their potential would remain untapped. The concept was well explained by an excerpt from a book written by Gene Bylinsky in 1976 called *The Innovation Millionaires: How They Succeed.* In this book he says, "Sam Wyly builds a highway for computers." And although I lost Datran, technology in the '70s kept moving forward at a rapid pace. The digital microwave towers

NET AMERICA

**Toll-quality satellite network services
at down-to-earth wholesale prices
for large-scale users**

- A satellite-based switched digital backbone network.
- Rates based on the user's *total* volume.
- Unique transmission plan with echo cancellation.
- Digital technology virtually end-to-end.

we had successfully made communicate between Houston and Chicago in Datran's late life were being replaced in the industry by commercially available satellites. Not yet ready to release my dream of connecting us by computer communication, in the early 1980s I created a new entity called NetAmerica. We spent four years and about $10 million engineering the technology for this company and concept. But again, the fates conspired against us. Wall Street was not receptive to the idea when we most needed it, and I had learned you need to know when to fold 'em.

& now ...

IF YOU LOOK AT COMPUTING and communication technology today, all of it is based upon a natural evolution of what we originally built at Datran. The services delivered by companies such as Google, Amazon, Apple, Microsoft, Facebook, and virtually all cloud software providers are reliant upon the transmission of data across fast, reliable, and affordable digital computer networks (both public and private) that are now global in scale. Even AT&T—the original telco monopoly—has transitioned its business to an almost entirely digital one, with most of its analog infrastructure being wound down as of the writing of this book. Despite these advances and the undeniable benefits that this now global data network has provided to much of the world's population, the promise has still not been fulfilled in many parts of the world, particularly in rural areas and in the developing world. Democratizing access to information is a moral imperative if we want to improve the standard of living for the more than four billion people that still lack reliable and affordable access to the Internet.

Seeing this challenge, my daughter Christiana's husband, Kimbal Musk, and his brother, Elon Musk, are deploying a global constellation of Starlink satellites via SpaceX vessels. These vessels will bring reliable, affordable, and scalable broadband access to underserved populations in areas in which terrestrial challenges—such as lack of adequate infrastructure, poverty, and political instability—conspire to prevent such access today. When we launched Datran, building a digital network between Houston and Chicago was a tremendous accomplishment. The current generation of entrepreneurs is now building upon our original mission and extending the promise of computer networks into new frontiers.

$115,000,000

Sterling Software, Inc.

8% Convertible Senior Subordinated Debentures due September 1, 2001

(Interest payable March 1 and September 1)

Price 100%

plus accrued interest from September 1, 1986

Copies of the Prospectus are obtainable in any State from the undersigned and such other dealers as may lawfully offer these securities in such State.

Drexel Burnham Lambert
INCORPORATED

September 2, 1986

RAISING CAPITAL

Sterling Software's $115,000,000 underwriting tombstone announcing
the capital raised to buy another software company. This was only two years
after Sterling Software's initial start-up funding with less than $1 million.

Play It Again, Sam

We wanted to be one of America's fastest-growing companies, to be one of the best investments, and to be a good place to work."

—Sam Wyly, *in* 1,000 Dollars and an Idea, *speaking about what motivated him to create his company Sterling Software, a bold reincarnation of his previous business endeavor UCC*

IT'S HARD TO PICTURE nowadays that at one time software wasn't a mainstream product, but back in the '70s Don Thomson and I would speak often about how important software would eventually become. In the early '80s, when IBM introduced personal computers, my theory was proven correct. Don and I started thinking we could resurrect UCC focusing instead on software products. First, we needed to build a team, so I reached out to Sterling Williams, who was my first service salesman at UCC back in the day. We didn't quite yet have a product, or customers, or a name—but he signed on anyways. I had a group of trusted individuals with whom to create a company, so next we needed to figure out what we were going to call ourselves. Don and Sterling suggested Wyly Software, but I replied with, "No, make it Sterling Software." Growing up, my mother would only buy the highest quality of sterling silver, never plated. She would rather have less

SAM AND DON
at Sterling Software

silver of a higher quality than more silver of a lesser quality. Sterling was a word to me that was synonymous with high quality, and that was what I wanted for our company—an association with quality. The goal was to curate and purchase software products. Don and I thought we could build a UCC 2.0, focusing this time on software rather than computing services. It was controversial thinking at the time, but we felt software revenue would become a bigger play than hardware and services revenue.

The timing was good. Software entrepreneurs were springing up everywhere. Don and I felt we could buy the best of these concepts and put them under our own one company umbrella and then find great talent to run the various entities. We didn't need to invent a product, we only needed to gather these great products that already existed. Upon owning the product, we would then take steps to enhance and improve that product. The first thing we had to do? Figure out what those companies were that we were going to purchase. We spent a year honing that list of potential purchases. We knew from UCC that application software was not as defined as systems software, so we decided to focus on systems. My team dug through thousands of software products looking for companies that would be a good fit. We prioritized, listed, evaluated, analyzed, and then we asked the ones we selected if they would care to be purchased by us. It was an unusual strategy, but I was always willing to march to my own beat, as were my partners, and the companies we approached were almost unfailingly receptive. We started buying up companies.

The primary criteria we applied to our evaluation of these companies were that (1) they needed to be important to IT departments across multiple industries and (2) have products that were IBM compatible. Growing a business by acquisition is not easy, but there are things you can do to keep it smooth. We always made sure the new employees were heard and incentivized to stay motivated in their jobs. We already had clear-cut plans as to what our vision was when we went into these companies, and sometimes that meant we sold part(s) of the companies we acquired. If this was the case, it was important to us that the sale be done quickly, and if that meant we needed to let go of any existing employees, we required they be well taken care of with generous severance.

FOLLOWING FOOTSTEPS
Laurie working for one of Sterling's companies, Dylacore, in California in the '90s.

We had a fully developed vision for every company we acquired, we presented it to their teams immediately, and then got on with selling software. We worked to empower each company to think of themselves as their own entrepreneurial segment of our greater whole, and we gave them full autonomy to run their business. I knew we were doing a good job because when we would come calling people didn't run; they wanted to hear what we had to say.

It was a time when there was an intrinsic risk to remaining a private company because the big boys could just blow you away or eat you up. Becoming part of our company would circumvent much of the danger these companies faced in trying to go public

BERLIN WALL
A picture of some of Sam's friends and most vital work partners, circa 1990, standing in front of the Berlin Wall. Pictured L-R: Eddie Lott, his wife Pat, Sterling Williams, his wife Barbara, then Werner Frank. Sam says of Werner, "In my later-day companies, Sterling Software and Sterling Commerce, Werner Frank, who emigrated from Germany to the US as an eight-year-old, became a significant contributor to the success of our company." He later wrote the book *Legacy: The Saga of a German-Jewish Family Across Time and Circumstances*, which was published in 2003.

themselves. We were not trying to absorb or eradicate or change any of these companies; quite the opposite, we wanted to keep each company as a separate entity, with their key personnel in place, and then give them the tools to better themselves while making everyone involved as much money as possible. It was not terribly different than Bonanza with family-owned franchises doing what they did best but benefitting from some corporate guidance from our team. There was a rhythm and a reciprocity, and most of it was easy. Only once was there a hostile takeover—when we took the side of one founder over another founder.

Warner Frank, who was a longtime industry associate, sought out both me and Sterling to present us with a company called Informatics. He was one of the founders, and at the time they, were the biggest com-

CASUAL FRIDAYS
Carol Morton, pictured center, was president of Dylacore and would ring a bell for every software sale Dylaclore made.

pany in the software industry. They were a $200 million company, and we were a mere $20 million company. Initially, Informatics wanted to purchase us. However, their reasons were not good or pure and although they were bigger, we knew from people both on the inside and out that we were much better run. Their interest in buying us seemed more like a threat from a playground bully who asked for your lunch money but was thinking he could take it if you didn't give it to him. I decided instead that we should buy them. It was a long process, and I knew it would not be easy. I don't like the way the phrase "hostile takeover" has seeped into our everyday lexicon, because the prevailing concept misses an important point–hostile to whom? If you treat the employees well, if you listen to them, if you keep your shareholders, needs and

GENERAL COLIN POWELL AND SAM
General Colin Powell stands with Sam at a Sterling Commerce technology conference prior to Sam's sale of the company to AT&T.

expectations in the forefront of your mind, if you are thinking of ways to optimize the product for your customer, if you create a better environment for all—then who is this so-called hostility directed at anyways? We entered into this endeavor with the intention to purchase this company, yes, but also with the intent to improve it, and we did both.

The best part of the Informatics acquisition was a tiny division called OrderNet that was renamed Sterling Commerce. It connected companies to suppliers to make ordering more accurate, faster, and less expensive. Sterling Commerce grew very quickly, and we realized the stock market would value this company greatly. We spun it off as a separate public company, and it became worth as much as all the other divisions combined.

Sterling Software purchased thirty-five companies over the course of seventeen years, and by the time we sold, the valuation was $8 billion when combining the sale prices of Sterling Software to Computer Associates and Sterling Commerce to AT&T. My initial investment had been less than $2 million. I knew from Datran I was not infallible, and I knew from Sterling that I had learned from my mistakes. Over the course of many years and many business endeavors the lessons of being adaptable, listening to my intuition, maintaining my optimism, and doing what I believed to be the right thing have helped me find my way to some very fruitful journeys.

then ...

AT THE TIME I started Sterling Software, software was still only an adjunct to a computer. IBM used to tack on software and throw it in for free, because the mainframe was everyone's focus. Realizing how specific software would grow and how many individualized needs it would be able to meet allowed me to be something of a trailblazer, just as recognizing there had to be a way to bring those out-of-reach computers to the masses inspired me to create UCC as a first business. When we are willing to look forward and explore solutions, rather than be mired down by what we perceive as the obstacles, there is a world of possibilities out there.

& now ...

IT HAS BEEN INTERESTING to watch the evolution of software since I sold Sterling to Computer Associates in 2000. The dominance of software accelerated in the decade afterward, as once proud hardware-first companies such as IBM, Dell, and HP found out the hard way. While many of these companies were able to pivot to newer business models in which their core business was supplemented by divisions focused on software, the writing had already been long on the wall when Marc Andreessen (cofounder of Netscape, one of the first web browsers, and now a well-known technology investor) made his famous comment that "software is eating the world" in 2011. Since that time, software has remained of paramount importance, but we have also seen the old model of licensed software taken over by the software-as-a-service (SaaS) model, in which software is delivered on a subscription and/or recurring revenue model instead of via licenses to customers.

In the same way that we pioneered the delivery of computer services at UCC and software product development at Sterling Software, today's technology entrepreneurs are using the internet itself as a platform for the distribution of their solutions—and not just to desktop/laptop computers, but to literally every device on earth via the Internet of Things (IoT). Additionally, two of the things that were core to our strategy at Sterling Software are now employed by not only the leading technology companies in the world but across virtually all industries: growth through strategic acquisitions and allowing those strategic acquisitions the autonomy to innovate while benefitting from the scale and financial stability of a larger parent company. I'm proud of the fact that many of the concepts and business practices we put into place years ago still guide many of the world's largest companies today.

When Getting Framed is a Good Thing

I remember my dad wanting to show me something. We drove down
Mockingbird Lane to a store called Michaels, and he asked me:

What do you see, Lisa?"

"I see an arts-and-crafts store, Dad," I responded after looking around.

"Yeah, well, I see a FULL PARKING LOT!" Dad said in response.

—SAM'S DAUGHTER LISA, *describing their first outing to
check out Sam's next investment, Michaels Arts & Crafts*

BACK IN THE EARLY '80S, I got word from a man named George
Griffin that a small arts-and-crafts store was going on the market.
I had known George since he was CFO and I was on the board at
Ling-Temco-Vaught, now known as Lockheed, which owned the giant
airplane factory in Grand Prairie. I was intrigued. I like photos and
I've gotten many of them framed, although that was the extent of my
exposure to craft stores. I've never cross-stitched a pillow or made a
friendship bracelet. But I saw the store's balance sheet, and it looked
good: Michaels had $4 million in cash and no debt. All the stores
had double-digit increases in sales. They were selling the chain for

TRICK OR TREAT
Sam and Don Thomson
stand beside a four-story tall,
inflatable gorilla at a Michaels
Halloween party which took place
at Sam's house on Beverly.

1997 MICHAELS ANNUAL REPORT
The picture on the cover is part of
Sam's personal art collection,
a painting that is now in the
Dallas Museum of Art.

$8 million. I saw a lot of potential. Plus, I saw that full parking lot. Clearly, there were a lot of crafty folks out there.

As I delved deeper into this potential purchase, I learned that the father and son who owned the store had a tumultuous relationship and were always fighting with each other—which made possible buyers hesitant, even scared them off. The father, Mr. Dupey, who hired George, wanted to sell and move to Florida. But the son, Michael, who had a profit interest in some of the stores and ran the warehouse, wanted to own the company.

I was told by people in the know that the son was a merchandising genius. He did all the buying and ran the distribution center and was almost savant-like in his ability to recognize, and also create, a crafting trend. This is the kind of talent you want to keep on board, and I began trying to plot out a way to make this work. I knew I needed some help figuring out how to proceed, and I knew just who to ask.

Part of good business is knowing when to get help. Over the years when I had found myself needing some guidance to turn things around, there was one guy who never let me down—Don Thomson. Some background on Don—he was a high school dropout who used to consider himself stupid, until an Army intelligence test revealed that he was actually dyslexic. Don was a brilliant man who had been dealing with a learning difference, and no one had recognized this. In the business world he proved his intelligence; he made a name for himself as someone who could take even the most complex problems and figure out solutions. He did that for me multiple times. The first time

EIGHTEEN WHEELER

A Michaels truck, parked in front of their only warehouse, with all of the store managers in the USA. Trucks arrived at each store two days a week with different products of the thousands that a customer could buy. As they grew they renamed the warehouse to "Distribution Center," and there were eight in America. This first one is in Irving, Texas, and the whole headquarters staff is on the front line. Sam is the "part-time guy" with the visitor badge (far right).

was at UCC; he came on board and he saw where we had opportunities to improve, where we required change, and how we could grow. It was his idea to turn software into a product. Don was an innovator, and he also liked a challenge. He didn't want a job where he could coast, he wanted to be working. So, once we had UCC running smoothly, he was ready to move on. Fortunately, the timing coincided with Bonanza needing some CPR, and so next Don joined me there. He looked at our financial statements, our locations, our menus, and more, and he found places for us to better our operation—appreciably. I knew when I faced some

When Getting Framed is a Good Thing   73

DON THOMSON, MR. FIX-IT

The best manager.

new unknowns at Michaels, I wanted to have Don by my side once again, and since he didn't like to stay anywhere too terribly long, once again the timing worked. Upon hearing about the problems with the store, Don said, "Don't worry—I can handle Michael!" And he did.

Since the first obstacle we had with Michaels was the father and son's relationship, Don and I negotiated a deal where we split the assets. We owned the business, but the son owned some of the most profitable stores in the Dallas metro area. The best part was he continued to run the warehouse for both his stores and ours, and we were able to utilize his buying genius for our mutual benefit. Unfortunately, he didn't care for Michaels' management much more than he did his father, so it wasn't always easy, although he

LOCATION, LOCATION, LOCATION
Doug Sullivan, a real estate genius who Sam credits for much of Michaels' success.

was always nice and professional in his interactions with me.

One of the things I learned during my Bonanza days was that real estate matters—a lot. By the late '80s, Michaels had grown from 6 stores to 105 stores. I needed a real estate mastermind to help us orchestrate our next moves, and I found one in Doug Sullivan. We continued to expand across the country, and there was a specific and well thought-out strategy behind every location we chose. We were opening fifty stores per year, almost one per week, with an incredible success rate. Doug would look at many different locations before choosing one, and he would create a competition between real estate developers as to who would get us. The developers knew if they had a Michaels on site it would drive a great deal of traffic

MICHAELS BOARD OF DIRECTORS
Sam's daughter Kelly, bottom right, was the only artist on the board.

to their location. Doug had a basic formula: we would not sign more than a ten-year lease and we would not pay more than $9 a foot. Doug was hugely responsible for Michaels' growth and profitability.

I also spent time inside the stores and inside our framing departments. I am a picture person, and the walls of my home are covered with photographs of friends, family, and places I love. All of these pictures on my walls are framed. As I observed the process of people bringing in their own personal memories to hang on their own personal walls, I knew what an important service we were offering.

I believe if you have someone in management who does something well, you best stand back and let them do it. When Mike Greenwood, the man who managed our custom framing department, said he wanted us to make our own frame molding rather than using suppliers as we previously had, I listened. We acquired a company that made framing materials for us to use, and we purchased a free-standing framing company called Aaron Brothers. The success was indisputable—we now had over 150 Aaron Brothers and over 900 Michaels country-wide.

During the ten years from 1984 to 1994 we opened new stores at the rate of 35 percent a year. We acquired LeeWards, another craft store and competitor, and that acquisition gave us 184 additional stores. Our growth strategy was aggressive and could be risky, but I believed in this plan of action and it paid off—in ten years we had grown to 380 stores and we were moving toward $1 billion in revenue. We had 442 stores by 1995. At this point, I needed a president for Michaels who shared my vision and could implement changes in operation that would maintain our growth. I knew that although our real estate locations were great, our supply chain, our merchandising, and our IT systems needed updating and improvement, and after extensive interviews, I found the man to do it—Michael Rouleau. He was tough and tenacious, thorough and detail-oriented, and direct.

MICHAEL ROULEAU
CEO of Michaels, and his wife Susan. Michael did a great job running Michaels for ten years.

Throughout those years of growing the stores at a breakneck pace, we had a very decentralized structure, because I knew that local managers could make better decisions than consultants or a distant corporate headquarter office. The people running the stores also needed to be the people who had the most direct contact with the customers. But with growth in size comes complications, and it was no longer feasible to maintain the total autonomy we previously had enjoyed. With the amount of inventory we had and the vast expansion we were experiencing, we had to develop a centralized system.

Prior to centralizing, store managers were placing their own orders and getting them shipped directly to their stores. The orders were not big enough to garner the best price, nor build the best relationships with vendors. But once we were ordering so much more product from a central headquarters, we had much more status and leverage. Additionally, before we centralized, we had no means by which to track inventory. There were tens of thousands of products in any given store, and the managers were having to eyeball them and make a best guess as to what was selling and what wasn't. There were many people in many markets making best guesses as to what to buy, so there were big inventory write-offs and also instances of under-purchasing, which led to loss of sales. Michael, who was with us for ten very profitable and gratifying years, opted for a well-deserved retirement in 2005. I was also ready to move forward. Michaels was a great twenty-plus year journey for me, but I was ready to sell. In 2006 we sold to Blackstone and Bain, a couple of Wall Street private equity firms, for $6 billion. It pays to diversify.

Sam Wyly sold the Michaels arts-and-crafts chain for $6 billion in 2006. The buyers sold it for $5 billion in March 2021 after holding it for fifteen years—a prime example of Sam's good timing!

then ...

WHEN WE first purchased Michaels, it came with some stores called Ben Franklin. These were five-and-dime shops and the predecessor to big department stores. These stores intrigued me because I knew long ago one was owned by a gentleman named Sam Walton. Prior to Walmart, Walton built his brand by utilizing the wisdom of an entrepreneur—listening to his customers and spending time on the floor. He changed the concept of retailing. Over the twenty years I owned Michaels, we had opportunities to evolve in ways I may not have anticipated, and much of our growth was because I emulated Sam Walton's model—I spoke with the people on the floor and I watched the customers. There is a personal aspect to a store like Michaels. There was a familial component to this business similar to Bonanza's, and just as it was gratifying to have a restaurant where people would come and bond with their families, I knew Michaels offered services that meant something to people, whether it was a mom baking with her children or a dad framing a picture. Part of being successful in business is digging deeper to recognize the reason that people come to your place.

& now ...

AS I WRITE THIS in 2021, we have had a long few months of sheltering in place during the COVID-19 pandemic. During the heights of lockdowns, the only businesses allowed to stay open were those deemed essential. Although we no longer own Michaels, I am proud to say it is one of those essential businesses. After so much time in the stores, I can see why. During this time, families have had time together like never before, and many of them have used this time to create and bond. Perhaps they build puzzles, create crafts together, or make art, but whatever it is, it speaks to the resilience of people. What is a very challenging time has been made easier and more enjoyable thanks to stores like Michaels that allow for this period to be so much more than simply feeling stuck. I know our country and our world will get back to normal and flourish again, but I am glad that during the challenges of this year, Michaels is recognized as essential because that is what art and creativity are—essential.

GREEN MOUNTAIN ENERGY WIND FARM
near Fluvanna, Texas. Note the cattle grazing beneath turbines, which are as high as a sixty-story skyscraper.

The Earth is Calling

"Choose wisely. It's a small planet."

—GREEN MOUNTAIN ENERGY *company slogan*

I AM NOT ONE WHO LIKES LABELS, and I will actively bristle when called an environmentalist. I have nothing against environmentalists, I just do not personally like to be categorized. That having been said, I believe we have an obligation to be stewards of this planet. The bad news is that in a short time we humans have done a lot of damage; the good news is we can repair and care for the earth and do so in a way that creates value and economic opportunity. More good news is that the awareness about our planetary responsibility has grown with every generation. When my daughter Christiana was in fifth grade in the early '90s she asked me, "What are we going to do about toxic waste?" Our children know we must clean up this planet. My daughter's innocent inquiry set me on a new trajectory with a new goal.

In 1997, in Burlington, Vermont, there was a small company called Green Mountain Power that had made it its mission to utilize the power of consumer choice to help create more clean air options for all. The company's founders believed that Americans should have the option to purchase clean energy to help protect our planet. I was interested in them because of their innovative and earth-driven mission. They were interested in me because in order to implement their

ALFRED MEMBRENO
a longtime family friend of the Wylys who drove the *Texas Got it Right* truck during book promotion. Standing beside him is a longhorn. It doesn't get more Texan than this!

mission they would need to go up against the utility monopolies—and they knew I had done this before. Going up against the big guy appeals to me on many levels, but what really appealed to me was the idea of giving Americans a choice between buying dirty or clean electricity. I felt if given the option, even if it was a little more money, many people would want to purchase clean. I believed that in the future, as natural gas and oil grew scarcer and technology improved, the cost of this clean energy would, in turn, continue to come down. We had the opportunity to educate consumers who cared about clean air. Initially our focus was on the residential market. Our research showed that 20 percent of customers would be willing to pay a premium for environmentally beneficial electricity. So, the idea was to break the monopolies, then benefit from that deregulation and build a national electric company based on clean energy.

In North America, we have three electricity grids: the Western grid, the Eastern grid, and the Texas grid.

Major North American Electrical Grids

TEXAS GOT IT RIGHT!

We were able to offer energy that was far cleaner than coal plants (the coal plants were dirty and ugly entities and needed to be eradicated). Since California was a deregulated state, we went there first. Unfortunately, their deregulation process and laws were poorly constructed. California allowed out-of-state electricity supply but set an extremely low price cap for electricity. As with most well-intentioned attempts to establish price controls, this artificially separated the free-market balancing mechanisms of supply and demand. Lacking the ability to effectively price our service based upon capital and cost of service requirements, and given the realities of the market, we realized that this was an uneven playing field and decided to pull out of the state. After that, we moved to Texas, which deregulated its electricity market in 2002. We set up our headquarters in Austin and embarked on making the world a greener place. Texas was the biggest electricity market in the country and also one of the nation's biggest polluters, in dire need of cleaner sources of energy. With Green

SAM'S BARN
in Colorado with its
impressive solar array.

SON EVAN IN GREEN
Sam's son Evan, an integral part
of the success of Green Mountain
Energy, stands smiling atop the
Santa Monica Mountains.

Mountain, customers now had a choice between an incumbent monopoly versus a company committed to benefiting the environment. Making electricity was the largest source of industrial air pollution in the US, and finally people could fight that with their selection of electricity provider.

Big plans require commensurate funding, and we needed investors. My son Evan became chairman and helped obtain initial investments from British Petroleum (BP) and Nuon, the Dutch electric utility, who each invested $50 million. The funding also came with the significant corollary benefit of a new chief executive officer, Paul Thomas, who had previously run the North American Gas & Power Trading Division at BP. He was a visionary and an activist, and as president he grew and expanded our clean energy portfolio to include not only wind, but also solar, geothermal, and biomass. I personally had solar installed on our barn roof in Woody Creek, Colorado, and at the time it was the largest photo voltaic installation in Colorado!

Paul helped us to develop a cooperative retailing program, which allowed us to work with incumbent utility companies in regulated markets to provide their customers with a green power option. This allowed Green Mountain to maintain their mission of offering environmentally friendly options to all—not just in deregulated markets. Utilities such as Portland General Electric and Florida Power & Light partnered with Green Mountain to offer green power to their own customers. We also pioneered a carbon offset program that is now global, with one offset representing the reduction of one metric ton of carbon dioxide or its equivalent in other greenhouse gases. Once the carbon footprint is established, an entity can purchase carbon offsets, with the revenue going to clean energy development to neutralize the company's footprint.

The mission of Green Mountain is still one of repair and healing this planet, and everything we did was to that end. I just happened to recognize that a goal of environmental consciousness could easily coexist with a profitable company, and by the end of 2007 the company had reached $300 million in revenue. By 2010, our revenue exceeded $500 million, and in September of that same year we sold to NRG Energy. I knew they would take our concept and use it to better the planet. I believe much of the success of Green Mountain came from a mentality that so many of us share that the time is now to make these changes. Getting rid of dirty coal was a great start, but it was only a beginning. People inherently want to do the right thing. If you provide them a better choice, they will take it, and the economics will follow. Just as I had suspected all those years ago, people want to have these earth-friendly options, and I am happy we were able to be a part of offering them.

CRAWFORD RANCH

(L–R) Sam, Lisa, George W., Laura Bush, and Charles Jr at Bush's Crawford Ranch in Texas.

WHEN "W" was co-owner of the Texas Rangers baseball team, we had seats nearby for our Sterling Software customers on first base. George W. Bush accomplished a lot as governor, including introducing me to Steve Wolens, head of the Democratic-controlled House of Representatives, who had a bill in the House which would deregulate Texas energy markets. George W. told me if I could help Steve get that bill through the House, it would pass the Senate, and he would sign it. Once he signed, this would deregulate the electricity industry in Texas—which would cut costs for homeowners and businesses and create jobs. This enabled Green Mountain Energy to offer "Clean Air through Clean Energy" as a choice for consumers and businesses.

then ...

MANY YEARS AGO, I realized that the best place for my energy company was Texas. The free-market mentality and bipartisan across-the-aisle cooperation meant we could move forward with what were then considered new and innovative concepts, such as giving people the option to improve the environment through their own purchasing decisions. Fortunately, these ideals have become much more the norm than the exception in terms of people having an expectation that they should have environmentally sound options available to them. Relocating to Texas was the reason Green Mountain was able to flourish, and we were able to make a positive impact on both the job market and the air quality, here in Texas and beyond.

& now ...

AS OF 2021, another big green giant will be moving to the Lone Star State. Elon Musk and his brother Kimbal are going to be bringing Tesla to an area right outside of Austin, not far from where we put our own Green Mountain headquarters. December 2020 was the first time Tesla's stock market value exceeded the nine largest automakers combined. This is despite selling only a fraction of the volume the other carmakers do. Travis County, where the car plant will be located, voted to give Tesla tax breaks of at least $14.7 million to build the plant, which will bring thousands of jobs to the area. Musk has referred to the factory itself as an "ecological paradise," with

TESLA ROADSTER

Evan and wife Kim were early supporters and buyers of Tesla's mission and products. Here they stand with car #507 out of 2,450 Roadsters that were made. Evan is still buying Teslas today and recently purchased their newest model.

a hiking and biking trail for all to enjoy. Musk has also referenced wanting to be in Texas where he can have the freedom to expand the way he wants to—which is very relatable to me after my experience with Green Mountain. Green energy should not be a hard thing to sell, but in some states, it is a very complicated and tricky proposition. Thankfully, Texas worked to facilitate an easier transition into a greener world when I was helping to deregulate electricity years ago and continues to do so today.

10

Making Maverick, an Adventure in Investing

Buy when there's blood in the streets. "

—Baron Rothschild, *an eighteenth-century British nobleman,
who spoke the credo for contrarian investing, a perspective Sam shares*

IN THE EARLY '90S, after selling Bonanza, I began partnering with my oldest son Evan on various investment opportunities. We didn't have any big business plan, just some shared interests as a starting point. I had money from Bonanza that I was looking to invest, and the research was always one of the most exciting parts to me. It was homework that I loved doing. It was an exciting time to be investing because the savings and loan crisis and the recession of 1990 created big bargains for those brave enough to weather the storm.

Evan and I had a different perspective from many of the typical investment people because our backgrounds were entrepreneurial and revolved around building companies. We looked at the strategy and the inner workings of companies and invested in those we believed would survive the turmoil and be long-term winners.

We started investing with $15 million in family assets (again, much of that coming from the recent sale of Bonanza). Since it was a very volatile time, we began investing opportunistically and found that junk bonds were a big bargain at the time. There was so much angst and negativity surrounding these bonds that many that had originally sold with a yield of 12 percent now had a yield of more than double that amount. They became a better bargain than ever for those who correctly chose which companies would make their payments.

Around this same time, Evan and I also began to investigate emerging markets in developing countries. Multinational markets had long interested me. Brady bonds were a then recently developed way to entice investors to invest in risky debt. We invested in debt in Latin America and Eastern Europe. Similar to junk bonds, high returns were available if you invested in countries that made their payments. Around this time, my overseas investment interests expanded to Asia.

Japanese equities were grossly overpriced, but Taiwan, Hong Kong, and Singapore were good places to be. As always, it came down to research for me, and we delved into learning about good growth companies and entrepreneurs. We found companies that were family controlled and honest. We did very well with this opportunistic strategy, but to evolve and expand, we felt potential investors would have more comfort with a less volatile, traditional hedged equity strategy.

In the beginning, Evan and I were just doing this for ourselves. We had some really good returns but were not necessarily thinking along the lines of a business. I liked to be diversified in my business interests, but diversified is a relative term. To me, it was having three or so businesses at once. For many people, diversified meant twenty investments. I felt that if I had three, and one performed poorly, then I still had the other two. But this investment work Evan and I were doing was performing very, very well. It was getting bigger than we had even anticipated. Now that this endeavor had shown promise, we wanted to continue on that trajectory and build something bigger still. Because of our belief that an organization is only going to be as successful as the people running it, we had a very deliberate approach to creating the infrastructure of our own investment company.

Evan and I knew that in order to do that, we would need to hire a portfolio manager with stellar stock selection skills. We started searching for this person who would help us take our concept to the next level. Richard Hanlon, who I had worked with off and on since my University Computing days twenty years prior, recommended a young man named Lee Ainslie, who worked at Tiger Management, one of the largest hedge funds in the world. Richard had interacted with many investment analysts as a senior executive at several large technology firms, and he said that of all the analysts, Lee had the best understanding and asked the most insightful questions. Evan and I always trusted Richard's advice and arranged to meet Lee. It turned out that Lee and I had very similar investment beliefs and perspectives.

As I have said before, I put a premium on intuition, and some of my best hires have bucked the conventional wisdom of who and what I "should" have been considering. Lee was young at twenty-eight and didn't really have his own track record since the Tiger portfolio manager, Julian Robertson, had the final say on stock selection. However, Evan and I were both impressed by Lee, his passion, his integrity, and his love of investing. On the flip side, we had to do some convincing on our end as well. Lee was working at Tiger, one of the best hedge funds in the world, and we were asking him to leave a great job, move west to Dallas, and start something brand new. Lee was well compensated at Tiger and required a large financial guarantee as well as a pathway to becoming the portfolio manager in order to make the move, so it was a big risk for him, and it was a big risk for us. It took some time, but we knew we found our man, and Lee moved to Dallas and came on board.

Next, we needed a name for our venture. Back then, it was just a startup without a company name or even a company office. As Evan says, "The early days were really fun because before Maverick formally started, it was just dad and me in our family office, picking stocks and bonds. When Lee came down to start Maverick with us, he and I sat squished in the conference room next to dad's office."

I wanted to name the company Bulldog in honor of my beloved college mascot. But Evan and Lee wanted Maverick. I am a history guy, and once I looked at the history of the word Maverick, I saw the allure. I discovered the word Maverick came from a rancher named Samuel Maverick who didn't brand his cows. He was one of the signers of the Texas

MAVERICK CAPITAL FIRST ANNUAL MEETING
Sam, George H. W. Bush, Lee Ainslie, Evan Wyly, and Charles Wyly stand
together at Maverick Capital's first annual meeting.

Declaration of Independence. Because he didn't brand his cows, when a cowboy found unbranded cattle on another ranch, they called it a "maverick" due to it not having a brand. Maverick meant someone who did not run with the herd and was a contrarian. I felt that fit us.

Our perspective on investing was fairly simple: invest in companies that are well run and likely to succeed and sell companies that are poorly managed and likely to fail. Evan stated our company goal succinctly and precisely: "to preserve and grow capital."

Although it was 1993 and common wisdom said to start slow, I felt the promise of great potential and was ready to move quickly. Evan, Lee, and I orchestrated an annual meeting at the end of the first full year, and I had my friend George Bush, who had just left the presidency, speak to our investors, or more likely, potential investors. We had it at a museum in Fort Worth that had a beautiful display of Chinese art, which I liked as a tie-in to our successes in China that year. Plus, George had at one time been the ambassador to China, so it all worked out quite well.

There were challenges. Potential investors would say they loved the concept, but they needed a five-year track record. Since we only had one year under our belts, that made it hard. We persevered, however, and the company flourished. Lee had a great strategy of being stock-centric and focusing on analyzing and researching the most fundamental aspects of the companies in which we wanted to invest. I knew that the company was in good hands with Evan and Lee, so before long I was ready to move on. I am happy to say Maverick has grown to become a respected firm managing $9 billion, creating rewarding careers and continuing to preserve and grow capital for investors.

then ...

WE USED TO HOLD roadshow presentations for our potential investors. This meant literally hopping on a plane to fly from Dallas to New York, London, Geneva, Zurich, or anywhere else we needed to go to share our strategy and performance with prospective clients and investors. We used old-school slide projectors with glass slides. While the touch factor was high, this wasn't a particularly efficient way to conduct business.

& now ...

WITH THE PROLIFERATION of the internet, video conferencing, and standardized presentation formats such as PowerPoint, Maverick can now communicate with investors virtually and at scale, regardless of geography or time. This has saved the most precious resource—time— and allowed an increase in the potential investment pool beyond our initial major financial centers. Overall, I would say this means of interacting today have resulted in a greater connectedness.

You Win Some, You Lose Some

11

"It ain't over till it's over."

—YOGI BERRA, *New York Yankees Catcher*

PART OF THE REASON I have done well as an entrepreneur and businessman over the span of my life is that I don't give credence to what people who don't know me think of me. It is important to me to do the right thing, and I would never knowingly hurt someone else. I had no interest in detailing my legal issues in this book, because it took up enough of my time while it was happening, and I am at peace with all of it. However, a lot of people have said they want to hear how it unfolded from me directly, rather than some of the variations that have been put out there.

Because this is a book about entrepreneurship, and this was part of my entrepreneurial experience, I am going to share it with you now, and if it helps anyone in their journey—great!

In 1992, I heard about an interesting tax deferral and estate planning idea involving annuities and offshore trusts. Instead of owning assets personally, some assets would be owned by offshore trusts, and this would provide more benefit to both my family and the many charities I support. A safe location for this trust was the Isle of Man, a self-governing British Crown dependency in the Irish Sea between Great Britain and Ireland. It would work like a 401(k), where the assets would grow tax deferred until retirement, and then I'd pay full taxes on the distributions, which I did. My taxes were paid at the highest rates, as I had given up the lower capital gains rates of earlier years.

The trust was the legal owner of the assets, so when the attorneys completed my SEC forms regarding the number of shares I owned in Michaels Stores, Sterling Software, and Sterling Commerce, they listed the number of shares that I owned personally, and they did not include shares owned by the trusts. My in-house lawyer, I'll call him lawyer #1, vetted the plan with the companies' lawyers, as well as other lawyers and accountants. The plan had been used by a lawyer in California (lawyer #2). Lawyer #1 had an estate-planning lawyer in Dallas (lawyer #3) do much of the work. Lawyer #1 also discussed the plan with a lawyer in London (lawyer #4), who called it "aggressive." I wasn't told about the comments of lawyer #4.

For fourteen years, the plan seemed to be working as expected. The companies had all been growing in value, which benefited all shareholders as well as the offshore trusts. I was surprised when the SEC announced an investigation in 2006 and a lawsuit in 2010 alleging violations of securities laws. The SEC argued in the many pages of filings that the trusts were not valid; that I should have included the trusts' number of shares in Michaels Stores, Sterling Software, and Sterling Commerce in the total number of shares that I owned personally. Which I would have been happy to have included! I was delighted to have big ownership in the companies I was leading. But I let the accountants and lawyers do what they do, and I was advised to omit this information. I was not sure why exactly the SEC would care. The rules are supposed to protect investors from scams where bad guys take advantage of investors to personally profit while the investors suffer large losses. However, in this case, no investors were harmed by not knowing the total number of shares. The SEC never showed even one investor losing so much as one dollar due to a lack of information. In fact, as you've seen elsewhere in this book, Michaels Stores, Sterling Software, and Sterling Commerce were all extremely successful and greatly benefited all shareholders.

Unfortunately, the trial was set in New York City, in front of a judge and jury who were biased against wealthy Southerners, particularly Texans. We had the first hint of that in a mock trial when a jury member said: "He (meaning me) must be a bad guy because people from Louisiana owned slaves." Another member said: "I don't think the SEC proved their case, but I don't believe people can get rich without cheating or stealing in some way."

Such blatantly biased comments were very hard to hear, but I still hoped that the truth would prevail. Interestingly, my defense attorney failed to mention that I myself had lived in Greenwich Village, New York, for many years, a place I loved and considered a second home. I would walk all over the village, visiting

MANHATTAN ISLAND

Manhattan was a home away from home for Sam. He spent many happy hours enjoying the city, walking along the Hudson River (on left), and building friendships with local New Yorkers. The perspective from which this photograph was taken (which would be high above the Statue of Liberty) offers a beautiful view of the island

the secondhand bookstores, making friends with the locals, and appreciating the culture of the city. I love New York, and my history there is quite expansive. In the 1960s, my family had an apartment in the Sherry-Netherland Hotel (song star Diana Ross was a neighbor) at the entrance to Central Park. At that time, I was raising capital for UCC. In the 1990s, we were back in Manhattan, but down near Washington Square, where I could walk over to the Hudson River. (Most locals believed that nothing important happened west of the Hudson, but the Hudson was also where Laurie and Lisa sailed to England with my mama aboard the *Queen Elizabeth II*!)

During this period, I was lucky to work with Ester Margolis and her New York-based Newmarket Press on my first book *1,000 Dollars & An Idea*. Broadway plays were close by, as was the place where my mama

had gone to a school of dance in the 1920s. I could go to church just two blocks up from my place. It was another home to me. In truth, given my relationship with the city, I was probably not nearly as unrelatable to the jurors as I was painted to be. Fortunately, the judge had a separate trial regarding a false allegation of insider trading and heard those arguments herself, without a jury, and we did win that.

In the jury trial about the number of shares, in addition to bias, another difficulty was the complex nature of SEC regulations. Pages upon pages of technical legal jargon were extremely difficult for a jury to follow. Unfortunately, the jury was swayed by the false tales spun by the SEC, and we lost that case. But how should the financial loss be calculated? Since no investors were harmed, there was no one to reimburse for losses. The SEC argued that the penalty should be

WASHINGTON SQUARE
Washington Square, where Fifth Avenue ends, is the beginning of Little Italy, an area settled by Italian immigrants when they first arrived. This is a special place for Sam, as he is deeply impassioned about the contributions of immigrants to America.

paid to the government and should be the amount of taxes that I would have owed, assuming the tax deferral plan and the trusts didn't exist. I wanted to appeal the $200 million judgment all the way to the Supreme Court if necessary, but I was advised by lawyers that it would take a very long time and that I should just make the payment, settle, and be done quickly.

Wanting to finish up all the legal issues, I filed for Chapter 11 bankruptcy protection in Texas to force the IRS to put up or shut up. This gave them a firm deadline to make a claim. With hindsight, I realize now that I should have appealed the New York case before starting the Texas process, because I was in the right and may have won the appeal, settling didn't make it go away quicker, and there were bad precedents that carried over to the Texas case against the IRS.

In 2015, the Texas judge was constrained by many of the decisions in the New York trial, and while I could have (and actually did) pay the amount of the taxes, the absurd amount of interest and penalties brought the total to $1.1 billion. The largest tax claim ever made against an individual. I joked, "This is an IRS billing error. They sent us Exxon's tax bill by mistake. Exxon's headquarters is a few miles from my house."

Unfortunately, the net result of all this federal government activity has been to waste the assets of America's citizens with less money going to taxes and charities and more to lawyers for the government and for legal defense. I would have donated much more to charity and probably paid much more in taxes had there been no federal government litigation.

While I had paid over $160 million in taxes over twenty-two years, and I'd agreed to pay an additional $200 million in taxes to the SEC settlement, I had to liquidate all my assets to pay as much as possible of the nearly $1 billion in interest and penalties. Ultimately, there was a settlement that will provide more than I'll need for the future. I'm grateful for my health and to have a nice place to live near a bunch of my kids and grandkids. It's also been gratifying to continue my work as an author (and I hope you're enjoying my writing!).

As I have said before: money is only one way to quantify a man's success, and certainly not the most important measure. Providing opportunities for others, giving back to the causes and the people you care about and believe in, and being able to look in the mirror and respect the person looking back—these are the real ways one can judge one's success in life.

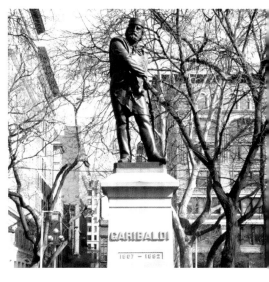

GARIBALDI STATUE
A statue of Garibaldi in Washington Square, near where Sam lived and attended church. Garibaldi was the "George Washington of Italy" just as Juarez was the "George Washington of Mexico."

then ...

As I have said, I still think fondly of New York, but it is where an agency of the federal government called the SEC (the "Short Seller Enrichment Commission" per Elon Musk) filed a lawsuit against me. There is a lot that could be discussed in terms of the precedents set by this case and the impact of those precedents. Again, in retrospect, I should have appealed the New York case. But instead, here is an example of "then and now" as it relates to me personally. Then, I lived in a huge house with an expansive yard. It was a beautiful house, and although it was over 10,000 square feet, I didn't use but 1,110 square feet of that space. It was more than I needed. Living there, I would spend time with my kids and grandkids, read my books, talk to my friends, and I would write—and things were good.

& now ...

As for New York, it is a city and a state that is losing people, businesses, and jobs (New York lost a congressman in the 2020 census, while Texas gained three congressmen in the 2020 census). It is not a state where jobs and people are moving to as they once did. As for me personally, I have downsized to an apartment-style home in a community living center. Rather than living in my 10,000 square-foot house that I only used 1,100 square feet of (save for various fundraising events through the years), I now live in an 1,100 square-foot space that I fully utilize. Living here, I spend time with my kids and grandkids, read my books, talk to my friends, and I write—and things are good!

Put Your Money Where Your Heart Is

12

Power, it's of no use unless you do good with it, like create jobs and opportunities for others to enrich their lives and those of their children."

—SAM WYLY, *from one of his previous books,* 1,000 Dollars and an Idea, *speaking to the opportunities and responsibilities that accompany wealth and power*

MOST OF MY LIFE'S WORK has been comprised of big business endeavors. I have owned and sold several companies and been fortunate to have created jobs for a great many people. One of the most gratifying business experiences I have had, however, also happens to be the smallest in scale.

As I have said, my love of reading shaped my life, and bookstores are among my favorite places in the world. I love all bookstores, small and large, and actively seek them out and spend time in them wherever I go. In Aspen, Colorado, where I had a second home, there was a much-loved local bookstore called Explore Booksellers. It sits in a Victorian house built in the 1800s. Much to the collective dismay of the

EXPLORE BOOKSELLERS & BISTRO
Sam, his wife Cheryl, and Jewely, one of their rescue dogs, sit outside the Explore Bookstore and Bistro.

town, it was put up for sale in 2006. Aspen is a literary town, and the locals are highly educated. Aspen is the only town of ten thousand people or fewer that has two different newspapers. Large chains and big-box bookstores have a lot to offer, but they don't have the character that this small, cozy, and quaint shop does. I always knew this place to be an important component of the town's history and identity, and I didn't like the thought of this small family business falling victim to another real estate developer who would no doubt be tearing it down to build condos for a wealthy contingency that would only occasionally be in town. So, in order to preserve this important part of the town's

SAM & SONS
Sam with his sons, Evan (left) and Andrew, enjoying Aspen.

culture, I opted to buy the bookstore myself. It wasn't a totally altruistic act. I spent a great deal of time in this place and fully enjoyed being there, so I was also doing it for my own benefit!

My decision to purchase came as a surprise to a great many locals who didn't fancy me the type to own this little bookstore, because I was a both a Texan and a Bush-backer (as in presidents—numbers 41 and 43). They didn't imagine me being the one to save this bookstore, which also had a vegetarian bistro housed in the attic space, but their incredulity didn't bother me. Aspen is a town of artists and creatives and intellectuals, and I wanted to support this place my family and I loved. One of the Aspen artists I speak of is my daughter Kelly O'Donovan, whose art gallery, the Elliott Yeary, is only three blocks away from the Explore Bookstore.

SAM & KELLY
Sam with his daughter Kelly.

WYLY ANIMAL SHELTER
Some of the lucky rescue dogs at the Cheryl and Sam Wyly Animal Shelter.

SAM & SETH SACHSON
Sam sits with Seth Sachson, signing copies of one of his previous books. Seth is the executive director of the Wyly Animal Shelter.

Upon purchasing the bookstore, I met with all of the employees to ask what I could do to help them and what they may need. At first no one replied, but then one of the workers asserted "We need a cat!" This was a convenient request, because right down the road was the Cheryl and Sam Wyly Animal Shelters. Cheryl and I were longtime animal lovers, and Cheryl's mom had been rescuing dogs in the Dallas area for years. We started flying the dogs to the shelter in Aspen where a young man named Seth Sachson was gifted at matching up pets and people. I was looking forward to having him find a cat for our new bookstore.

I purchased the Explore Bookstore for $5 million with the intention to save it. Years later, I sold it for the exact same amount to someone I knew would also honor that objective. I am happy to say the store still stands there today.

then ...

OVER FORTY YEARS AGO Explore Booksellers was established by Katherine Thalberg. When her daughters decided to sell it, it was as if a piece of the town's history was going to disappear. My wife Cheryl and I didn't want to see that happen, so we purchased it ourselves in order to preserve it. Even then small businesses were starting to be an endangered species. Sometimes you make an investment because it makes sense in your head, other times you make an investment because it makes sense in your heart—this was the latter.

& now ...

PRESERVING HISTORY is more important than ever. Both the historic Victorian home Explore is in and the unusual books inside of it draw visitors from all over when they come to Aspen. Times have changed, and now books are available electronically and that, in conjunction with the huge bookstores of the world, has threatened the survival of independent bookstores like Explore Booksellers. But this particular place is an institution in the town of Aspen and contributes to the overall culture.

follow your heart

DRAGONFLY
A hover test of *Dragonfly*, a test vehicle, in McGregor, Texas,
at the SpaceX rocket development facility.

13

IN CONCLUSION

(By Sam's daughter, Christiana Wyly Musk)

The Sky is the Limit

Shoot for the moon. Even if you miss it,
you'll land among the stars."

—NORMAN VINCENT PEALE

10 . . . 9 . . . 8 . . . 7 . . . 6 . . .

WHILE THE WORLD WAS SHOUTING the final countdown in unison, the control room of Launch Complex 39A at NASA's Kennedy Space Center in Cape Canaveral, Florida, was entirely silent. The fifty or so masked operators and spectators held their breath while gazing out the tall glass windows facing the steaming rocket in the distance.

This was not my first rocket launch, but it was by far the one with the highest stakes. This time, two US astronauts were sitting aboard the Dragon rocket, ready for a high-speed ride to the International Space Station (ISS).

The launchpad was initially built to send astronauts to the moon; eventually it evolved into the departure point for space shuttles lifting off into Earth's orbit, including the historic Apollo missions. But America had not launched astronauts from US soil in over a decade. However, on May 30, 2020, the U.S. government put their faith in SpaceX to deliver Doug Hurley and Bob Behnken safely beyond the bounds of our little blue planet.

From where I was standing in the back of the control room, my husband Kimbal's Resistol cowboy hat stuck out as he stood nearly smack in the center front of the room, next to his brother Elon. Rocket scientists and engineers aligned on either side, monitoring up-to-the-second data on the rocket's complex systems, the life support of the pilots, and nuances of the weather at every level. They whispered updates inaudibly into their mouth pieces.

My husband says he wears the cowboy hat because it reminds him that he is living the American Dream. Today we live in Boulder, Colorado, named the Happiest City by *National Geographic*, where each day we enjoy walking in the sunshine along the Rocky Mountains amongst the wildflowers. After a career in tech, Kimbal now runs a family of restaurants that are on a mission to create community through food. Three of his restaurants lie in the heart of Boulder's iconic red-bricked Pearl Street—The Kitchen Bistro, Next Door Eatery, and Upstairs Cocktail Lounge. He also helps his brother Elon grow Tesla, whose mission is to accelerate the world's transition to sustainable energy; and SpaceX, whose vision is to ensure humanity becomes an interplanetary species.

Born in 1972 in Pretoria, South Africa, during apartheid, living behind bars of a gated middle-class house was not enough to protect Kimbal from the terrors of urban Africa. Kimbal felt there was little very little regard for human life. As a teenager he went to the protests to meet other people who also believed a better nation and better world was possible. A world free of racial oppression and in which everyone had equal rights and pathways for opportunity.

Despite his love for the bushveld where he thrived in the wild among the giraffes, elephants, and the pesky baboons we often associate with Africa, he was in a hurry to get off the continent at eighteen. Upon graduation from high school, he had received a letter to show up for duty in the South African Army as a "field engineer," which entails crawling on one's forearms through the bush stabbing a hand knife into the ground to identify the location of landmines. He knew that this role had the highest probability of death in the army, which did not align with his big dreams of building a better world.

Thanks to their mother's birth in Moose Jaw, Saskatchewan, both Kimbal and his brother Elon had Canadian citizenship, and a year earlier, Elon had used his to attend Queens University in Kingston, Ontario. That sounded better to Kimbal than death by landmine, malaria, or jungle militia.

The brothers were grateful to live in a place so safe that the homes had no bars on their windows and enjoyed their quality education in Canada. They knew that America was the only place to go after college to start a company that would help create the internet. But getting to live and work and build a business in America was not easy.

They arrived in Palo Alto with little savings and modest start-up capital from an investor who believed in their concept for an online door-to-door mapping platform called Zip2. They were so short on cash, they had to choose between renting either an apartment or an office, so they opted for the office, since sleep was a scarce commodity anyhow. When they did find time for sleep, it was either on the floor or futon couch

SPACEX ROCKET LAUNCH
SpaceX launches at NASA's Kennedy Space Center in Florida.

at the office. They would shower at the YMCA and traveled by bus around Silicon Valley to pitch venture capitalists on their vision to make the yellow pages and paper maps obsolete. But even after having sold Zip2 to Compaq for $300 million, they still had to fight hard to stay in the country.

Today, Elon and Kimbal Musk are proud to call themselves Americans. They are proud, as a family of immigrants, to have the opportunity to serve their country by building rockets for NASA.

5 ... 4 ... 3 ... 2 ...

The room began to shake like the California tremors I had become accustomed to in my childhood. I resisted the reflex to seek cover as the black smoke billowed from the base of the rocket. This was the most dangerous moment, when the rocket itself could become a firebomb pulsing out across the horizon, evaporating all life in its path. But instead, the Dragon craft climbed higher and higher, angling up through the gray sky, finally piercing the clouds and moving beyond our view.

The day of the Dragon rocket launch, the rain showers continued to pass over us as they had for our entire hour-long drive from our little house nestled in the everglades, where we had been quarantined from the coronavirus while waiting for our launch window. Unlike the Tesla windshield in the car ride over, these giant windows had no wipers to clear our view, and the rain washed down the surface of the glass in sheets. But rain on our windows was not as significant as lightning at higher levels in the atmosphere, a factor which had resulted in a cancellation of the launch four days earlier a mere thirteen minutes before blastoff. The astronauts had to be removed from the rockets and placed back in quarantine just like the rest of us. We had spent the time together as a family in the sweltering Florida spring, waiting for the moment we could return to 39A and resume the countdown.

Still, the room was silent. We could not cheer until the vessel had separated safely from the boosters, moved beyond the Earth's atmosphere and situated itself in perfectly aligned orbit to meet up with the ISS. This occurred twenty minutes after the blast, at which

KIMBAL MUSK

Sam's son-in-law, Kimbal Musk, stands with his sister Tosca (on left), and his mother Maye, under the belly of the Dragon Rocket.

point the room finally erupted in mask-muted cheers and socially distanced "air hugs."

Nineteen hours later, Behnken and Hurley stepped onto the space station, where they would remain until their splashdown on August 2, 2020. It was not until then, when the four red-and-white parachutes opened like giant jellyfish elegantly dropping the astronauts into the Gulf of Mexico that the mission would be considered entirely successful. As Neil Armstrong said when he took the first step on the moon—"One small step for man, one giant leap for mankind."

The next giant leap for mankind is leveraging the space platform to bring high speed internet to everyone in the world. I am proud that my family has already played a meaningful role in the evolution of information communication. Telecommunication is the transmission of information by various types of ever-evolving technologies, going back as far as the smoke signals and drums that originated in Africa. Homing pigeons in Persia were adopted by the Romans and utilized all the way until the nineteenth century. The Greeks developed semaphore to display visual symbols powered by water pressure. However, the modern telecom industry ignited when powered by electricity, and evolved from the mid-eighteenth century through today from transmission over wire in telephone, and radio to other electromagnetic systems.

Beginning in the 1960s, my father Sam helped build the telecommunications foundation for what became the internet. He and his brother Charles led the wave from computer hardware to software and enabled the creation of communication superhighways by breaking down the monopolies that prevented innovation.

My husband and his brother picked up where they left off, helping build the first generation of the internet. Both sets of brothers sold their internet companies in 1999, (the year that I graduated from high school), just before the great crash of the dot-com boom.

The early 2000s saw the beginning of the next wave called Web 2.0, which was an interactive social sphere, where people engaged with one another across various platforms. Elon created PayPal, which enabled money payment online, and I made a small contribution with Zaadz.com which became a place for people to meet like-minded others across the world and exchange ideas.

Today, 48 percent of our global population of 7.6 billion has access to the Internet—an exponentially increasing network of the world's collective knowledge. But that still leaves more than half without the ability to either learn from or contribute to the collective. In America alone, 19 million people still lack access to fixed broadband service at threshold speeds. But that is soon to change.

SpaceX is launching a constellation of thousands of small satellites called Starlink that will deliver high-speed broadband internet to locations where access has been unreliable, expensive, or completely unavailable. At the time of this writing, 540 of 42,000 satellites have been launched on SpaceX vessels targeting service in the northern part of North America in 2020. We hope to expand to global coverage of the populated world by 2021.

When I look back at how innovations in telecommunications have shaped society, enabling connection across divides in distance, language, and cultures,

THE LITTLE PRINCE

The Little Prince was a favorite book of Christiana's that Sam used to often read her before bed. It was a prescient story to share based on the important role outer space would play in their lives.

Here is my secret. It's quite simple: One sees clearly only with the heart. Anything essential is invisible to the eyes."

—Antoine de Saint-Exupéry,
The Little Prince

I am inspired to imagine what advancements in our collective consciousness will emerge when the other half of humanity comes online. My hope is that in the near future, access to education and information will be equitably distributed and accessible to all so that we can find all the bright lights and young minds and empower them to become leaders of the future. Can we harness the collective wisdom of humanity toward shaping a future that is more peaceful, healthy, and sustainable for all? Breakthroughs in information communication, food and energy systems, and transportation are critical pathways for shaping that future, and I am proud to be a member of two families who are leading the way.

Christiana Wyly Musk
—Christiana Wyly Musk

Top Ten Lessons from My Mentor

Our chief want in life is somebody who will make us do what we can."

—RALPH WALDO EMERSON

MY FATHER-IN-LAW, SAM WYLY, has been a wonderful role model and mentor. He is truly the inspiration for my venture capital company, RevTech Ventures, inspiring our mentorship model and the eponymous Sam Wyly Conference Room. Having more than thirty years of membership in his extended family, I've realized that his entrepreneurial gifts are unique and special. If I can emulate just one percent of what I have learned from him, it will be satisfying. After all, one percent of his example would mean creating more than a dozen newly minted millionaires, generating over $300 million of shareholder wealth, creating over 2,000 jobs, and giving more than $5 million to charitable endeavors. I'd be happy with that! Here is a summary of what I have learned from Sam through the last three decades, and I hope it helps and inspires you the way it has me.

HISTORY REPEATS ITSELF

It is hard to remember a conversation with Sam where the subject of history has not come up–specifically American history, and even more specifically, American history through the lens of the Wyly family genealogy. I would often wonder for example, "What does this story about his great-uncle's experience during the Civil War have to do with today's topic at hand?" Gradually, I began to realize that the student of history has a certain advantage when looking at future trends, for history tends to repeat itself.

How did Sam know that oil would peak in 1980? How did he know that the breakup of the AT&T monopoly would spur massive telecom innovation in the 1980s and 1990s? How did he know that renewable energy and energy deregulation would begin to accelerate in the late 1990s? How did he know it was time to sell his technology stocks in late 1999? While contemplating these market movements, he was most certainly applying what he had learned from history.

UCC COMPUTER UTILITY
A picture of the headquarters of Sam's first company, University Computing Company. "Computer Utility" was a term Sam coined to refer to the marriage of the telephone and the computer, long before the word Internet existed.

MONOPOLIES KILL INNOVATION
(Therefore, Kill The Monopolies)

Sam never feared a monopoly. His is a very David-vs-Goliath story. After leaving IBM (which had a near-monopoly in computing until the 1960s) he found a way to thrive with a computing services company called University Computing Company, or UCC. When AT&T's telecom monopoly crushed his first, all-digital computing network called Datran in the late 1970s, he was one of three companies that persevered to win an anti-trust lawsuit that broke up the monopoly.

I remember Sam telling me as early as 1990 that state-regulated electricity companies would some-day have their monopolies broken up and I thought, "What is he talking about?!" But there he was with Green Mountain Energy, just eight years later, taking on the electricity monopolies in California, Texas, and other states.

"SUCCESS IS THE QUALITY OF THE JOURNEY"

Thanks to the success of UCC, Sam was a millionaire by age thirty and a billionaire by age sixty-five, but he took it all in stride. In fact, he measured success by what he did for other people—millionaires enabled, jobs created, impactful philanthropy—and not by his accumulation of investments, homes, and airplanes. That all happened as a happy by-product of bringing great ideas to fruition. In an adverse tax ruling in 2014, when the federal government's IRS sent him the largest tax bill ever assessed to a private citizen, he responded by saying, "It's a billing error—they meant it for Exxon whose HQ is in the nearby town of Irving." This ruling in substance tested his estate plan for his children, and it was not found wanting. The family was protected. The large fine only accomplished diverting monies that would have gone to education and charities.

SURROUND YOURSELF WITH THE BEST PEOPLE
(And Do Not Cap Their Success)

Sam has a remarkable gift for recruiting and support-ing the best people to manage his software companies, restaurant chain, retail chain, energy companies, and hedge funds. When people introduced him to the right talent, he knew it immediately and gave each

WYLY THEATRE DEDICATION
Some of what incentivized Sam to be a part of this project was that the theater resides on a street named Flora, which was also his mom's name. As Sam's mom cultivated his passion for the arts, the street name was quite serendipitous.

WYLY THEATRE
The Wyly Theatre in downtown Dallas Arts District is one of the most versatile theatrical performing venues in the world.

of them an uncapped opportunity to reach for the stars. He also knew when it was time to sell a company and was able to persuade most of these managers to cash in their chips when the time was right.

One of the most remarkable examples of this was in 1996, when he convinced Sterling Williams, the CEO of Sterling Software, that spinning off the company's crown jewel—the e-commerce division which became Sterling Commerce—would be worth more than the sum of the parts. Sure enough, a company worth $2 billion in 1995 became worth $4 billion plus $4 billion by March 2000.

SHARE YOUR SUCCESS

How many entrepreneurs, business managers, artists, educators, managers of charitable organizations, and extended family members have benefited from Sam Wyly's largess? Thousands!

GIVE BACK TO YOUR COMMUNITY

It is plain to see Sam's emphasis on education, given that the majority of his philanthropy has gone to education. His first big gift was the Wyly Tower of Learning at his alma mater, Louisiana Tech, the tallest building in Ruston, Louisiana. Since then, there's been Wyly Theater at Alcuin School, Wyly Auditorium at Lakehill School (a gift from his brother, Charles), Sam Wyly Hall at the University of Michigan, and many other gifts. Wyly Theatre, in the Dallas Arts District, was a gift from Sam and Charles in remembrance of their talented mother, Flora (Flo Flo) Wyly. He was also one of the principal donors to Thanks-Giving Square, a unique commemoration to the importance of gratitude in downtown Dallas. In total, his philanthropy has totaled more than $500 million over the past fifty years.

ACCENTUATE THE POSITIVE, ELIMINATE THE NEGATIVE (And Do Not Waste Time on the In-Between)

Sam Wyly does not waste time with negativity; there is simply no room for it in his worldview. What a great example! Think how much precious time is wasted on negative thoughts and actions. From boyhood, Sam focused on achieving positive goals, including earning the rank of Eagle Scout, winning the state championship for his high school football team, and being elected president of the Louisiana Tech student body.

In business, a threat or challenge is often actually an opportunity in disguise. This type of opportunity can be extremely hard for even the best of managers to see. Many leaders, especially male leaders, see a threat and are predisposed to fight it out. It requires an unusually positive attitude to push that instinct aside.

Here is a great example of Sam's opportunistic vision: In 1999, Green Mountain Energy engaged a leading underwriter to cash in on the dot-com bubble and complete an initial public offering (IPO). The massive influx of capital to dot-com startups, pitching market land-grabs ranging from apples to zippers, had peaked early in the year. By summer, the flood of dollars began to wane, and Sam realized he may have missed the window. Did he despair? No! He

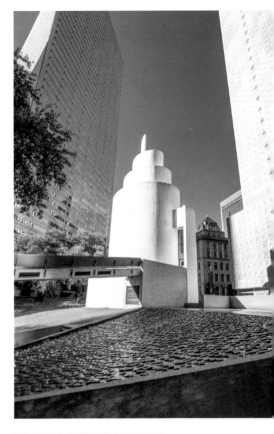

THANKS-GIVING SQUARE
landscaped garden and nondenominational chapel building in Downtown Dallas.

immediately convinced the boards of both Sterling Software and Sterling Commerce to sell while the getting was good. The result was that Sterling Software sold to Computer Associates for $4 billion and Sterling Commerce sold to SBC Communications (now AT&T), also for $4 billion. They completed these exits just days before the NASDAQ peaked at 5,000 and then imploded. Green Mountain Energy turned out perfectly fine as well; the investors doubled down and achieved their successful exit ten years later, when the company was acquired by NRG.

THINK BIG AND FOCUS!

Each of Sam's diverse blockbuster successes began with a bold vision. With his first company, UCC, he envisioned the big idea and led the charge to capture it. With each of his following companies, though, he had the big vision and recruited the CEO that could best execute on the strategy.

At Sterling Software, an enterprise software company that competed directly with Computer Associates (CA), it was Sterling Williams, one of his top lieutenants, who had managed sales at Sam's previous software company, UCC, who executed the strategy. Sterling Software was an aggregator of smaller enterprise software companies. It began with a $20 million IPO that funded the exercise of four options to acquire four different software companies. The day before the IPO, it was a company with $0 revenue; the day after the IPO it was a company with $20 million revenue. From the initial acquisition of the four companies, the company went on to make twenty-nine more acquisitions over the next seventeen years.

SAM AND DAVID
In 1982, Sam bought a controlling interest in Michaels stores. He had eleven stores that had a revenue of $10 million, Sam took them public in 1984, and today there are 1,250 stores, amassing over $5 billion in sales. On a 1994 visit to mainland China, Sam and Laurie's husband, David, went to see the factory that produced silk flowers for Michaels.

At Michaels, the largest arts and crafts specialty retailer in North America, several interim leaders headed the company during the first ten years of Sam's controlling ownership. Then, after a disastrous year in 1995, a headhunter introduced him to Michael Rouleau, an ex-Lowe's executive. Rouleau jumped at the chance to go from second or third in charge at a large retailer to head honcho at a smaller, specialty retailer. Ten years later, Sam sold the company to Bain and Blackstone Private Equity for a $6.5 billion leveraged buyout.

At Maverick Capital, a hedge fund that Sam co-founded in 1990 with his eldest son Evan, he recruited one of the "tiger cubs" from one of the most well-known hedge funds of that time, Tiger Management. Maverick Ainslie (just kidding, his first name is Lee) jumped at the chance to go from second or third in charge at Tiger Management to the investment team lead at Maverick. Ainslie went on to grow the assets

DAUGHTER LAURIE
A picture of Sam's daughter Laurie. Laurie was in Kaohsiung, Taiwan, teaching English as a second language in 1989 when Sam came to visit her.

under management to $10 billion at the firm's peak. They are still doing well today, thirty years later.

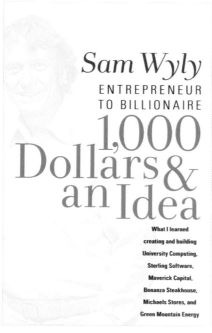

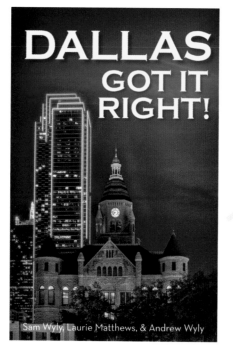

ALWAYS BE LEARNING

Sam has always been an avid reader and has proven many times over the ability to become a subject matter expert on multiple industries. I had the amazing opportunity to witness this as he willed Green Mountain Energy into existence in the late 1990s. Sam amassed incredible knowledge about the utility industry, about the legislative process for utility deregulation, about renewable energy and its generation and distribution, and about the entire electricity ecosystem. I was pleased to play a bit part in developing a successful affinity marketing model for Green Mountain Energy, and I was coached significantly by Sam during this process.

Sam is such an avid reader that when his favorite bookstore in Aspen was in danger of closure, he bought it! Not surprisingly, in his retirement he has transformed from entrepreneur and financier to author.

DO RIGHT AND FEAR NOT!

As you have hopefully discerned by now, Sam has a courageous exuberance that does not know failure. Whether it's leading his football team to the state championship, breaking up an entrenched monopoly, or defending his estate plan against the US government, he has a bold vision, the confidence that his plan is founded on principle, the willingness to recruit and support the best managers, the tenacity to persevere through the ups and downs, and the consistent focus to keep moving the ball toward the goal line. When he's won, he's invariably already been two steps ahead in working on the next big idea; when he's lost, he's cheerfully picked himself up and continued on.

In summary, what have I learned from this amazing mentorship over the past thirty years? I have learned to recruit great people, to lead by example, to not forget my humble roots, to follow the Golden Rule, to have a thicker hide (still working on that one), to try to do right by people, and to enjoy the journey! While still striving to achieve that one percent of Sam's success, I am well on the way.

DAVID AND LAURIE MATTHEWS

David Matthews

—David Matthews

THE GOLDEN RULE

A universal rule of ethical conduct is to treat others as you want to be treated,
"Do unto others as you would have them do unto you."

Acknowledgments

WE WOULD LIKE TO THANK Abra Garrett for her help with interviewing and editing. She facilitated the creative process with brilliance, skill and joy.

Also, a big thanks go to Anita Stumbo for her graphic design talents. She was such a delight to work with, and she helped make the swirl of ideas more concrete.

Another integral person to the completion of this book is Evan Wyly. Whenever there was a stalling of activity or any resistance along the way, he helped get us moving along.

And finally, thanks to a great entrepreneur in the book business, Milli Brown, and her team at Brown Books Publishing Group & The Agency at Brown Books.

Index

Photo Credits

Family Trip, Jim Paussa   vi

Louisiana State Capital, Berkomaster/Shutterstock   11

The Great Debaters, Moviestore Collection/Alamy   13

William Andrew Paton, University of Michigan   17

David vs Goliath, VectorFrankenstein/Shutterstock   22

Boston Copley Square Statue, Ingfbruno/Wikimedia Commons 28

SMU Dallas Hall Shaunnol/Wikimedia Commons 32

Starlink, CG Alex/Shutterstock   54

Wind Farm, Leaflet/Wikimedia Commons 80

Alfred Membreno, Alfred Membreno   82

Sam and Andrew, Karen Sanders   83

Son Evan in Green, Karen Sanders   84

Yogi Berra, Bowman Gum/Wikimedia Commons 96

Manhattan Island, TierneyMJ/Shutterstock   100

Washington Square Park, Agnieszka Gaul/Shutterstock   102

Statue Garibaldi, Elias H. Debbas II/Shutterstock   103

Sam and Cheryl, Jim Paussa   106

Sam, Evan and Andrew, Karen Sanders   107

Dogs, Bland Nesbit   108

Sam and Seth Sachson, Kelly O'Donovan   108

SpaceX Dragonfly, SpaceX Photos/Wikimedia Commons 110

SpaceX Rocket Launch, Geopix/Alamy   114

The Little Prince Looking At The Stars, Denmorganstudio/Shutterstock   118

Wyly Theater, Dorti/Shutterstock   122

Thanks-Giving Square, F11Photo | Dreamstime   123

All other photos are from Sam Wyly's personal collection or public domain.

About the Authors

SAM WYLY'S journey from the small towns of Lake Providence and Delhi, Louisiana, to the heights of entrepreneurial success is a captivating one. Although he knew some challenging times while growing up (including living for a while in a plumbing-free cabin on the lake), Sam was raised in a loving and supportive family, and attended school where he excelled in both sports and academics. When he was in high school, Sam's parents purchased *The Delhi Dispatch*, the local paper. This gave him an unusual opportunity for a young man his age—writing for a newspaper, thus solidifying early a lifelong love of authorship. He also played on the high school football team, a team which won the state championship—thus solidifying early a lifelong love of football. In college, he was Head Page in the House of Representatives in Baton Rouge, and at Louisiana Tech he was President of the freshman class as well as Student Senate. Sam's interest in politics never wavered, and to this day he remains invested in various political causes that are close to his heart. As the first ever Paton Scholar at the prestigious University of Michigan, he received an MBA before relocating to San Antonio to serve in boot camp for the Texas Air Force National Guard. Upon completion of his service, Sam began working at IBM, and from there took on a couple more corporate positions before his indisputable destiny as an entrepreneur became clear.

While entrepreneurial success is often chalked up to luck, in Sam's case, this is only true if that term is defined, in the words of Vince Lombardi, as "what happens when preparation meets opportunity." Sam's preparation was a voracious appetite for knowledge, combined with a historian's acute observation skills and the application thereof to broader social, political, cultural, and, of course, economic trends. In the same way that science fiction writers have at times uncannily predicted what would happen many years later, Sam's foresight in predicting the future of multiple different industries led to the creation of companies that were well ahead of their time.

University Computing was cloud computing before the proliferation of the internet. It was the predecessor to some of the world's largest companies today—most notably Microsoft, Amazon, and Google—in applying economies of scale and distributed processing to the world of technology. He then further evolved that model with Sterling Software, making code paramount to hardware, a trend that persists to this day.

Michael's Stores—a retail business in an industry that seems entirely dissimilar to high tech—was a precursor to the DIY ethos of creative self-expression that is seen today. It is relevant not only in the retail world, but also in the online world, on sites such as Etsy, Pinterest, TikTok, Instagram, and virtually every platform that enables individuals to express themselves through many mediums.

Green Mountain Energy was the pioneer in providing green power to ecologically conscious consumers, and helped to propel energy market investments in these same technologies forward. Today, out of all carbon emitting sectors of the US economy, it is perhaps not surprising that the one that has made the most impact in reducing its impact on our Earth is the power sector—driven largely by what Sam put into motion at Green Mountain Energy. Today, we see the same efforts applied to the transportation and materials sectors, and we can only hope for similar results.

While the end result of these innovations has undoubtedly had innumerable societal, economic, and functional benefits, it should be noted that what drove Sam's investments was solving gaps in these markets that were not being addressed by incumbent solutions. Preparation met opportunity, and the world has been the luckier for it.

These are but a few examples of the accomplishments Sam can

count and the companies he has built. Over the years, Sam's businesses have created over 200,000 jobs, and his work has helped many individuals to become millionaires. His love of business and innovation is second only to his love of family, and Sam proudly claims six children, twelve grandchildren, and ten great-grandchildren. Sam is the author of multiple other books, including *Dallas Got It Right, Texas Got It Right, The Immigrant Spirit,* and *1,000 Dollars and an Idea.* Today, Sam resides in Dallas, Texas, where he reads, writes, walks, and spends time with friends and family.

• • •

LAURIE MATTHEWS, wife, devoted mother of three, and community volunteer, like her twin sister Lisa (as well as her other two sisters and two brothers) feels quite lucky to be part of the Wyly family. Growing up, support was plentiful, conversation was lively, and opportunities were bountiful. Laurie was born and raised in Dallas but left the great state of Texas to attend college, along with her twin, at Principia in Illinois. There, Laurie majored in Business Administration with a minor in Small Group Communications. Upon graduating, she worked a short time as a Christian Science nurse before traveling to Kaohsiung, Taiwan, to teach English to children. After moving back to the states, Laurie and her husband, David, lived in California, where she worked for one of her father's companies. There she did her best to not let it be known she was Sam's daughter, as it was important to her to be treated like all the other employees, although this was the type of information that could only be kept quiet for so long. As much as Laurie enjoyed living in different parts of the world, when it came time to have a family of her own, the allure of being back in Dallas, with her own parents and siblings, was too strong to resist.

Returning to Dallas, she settled easily back into the city she grew up in and enjoyed raising her three children close to family. She was an active volunteer in their children's Montessori school, where she served on the Parents' Club and then on the school board, where she acted as president. Although church and volunteer commitments took up a great deal of her time, she collaborated with her father and brother, Andrew, authoring a book entitled *Dallas Got It Right*. Having discovered her love of writing, co-authoring this book with her father and twin was a true labor of love.

Composition of *Beyond Bubba* began in February of 2020, and although the pandemic provided numerous obstacles, the three Wylys worked through these challenges with their usual fortitude and positivity. The mandatory slowing down of the world allowed time for delving deeper than ever into Sam's history and the multitudes of lessons that accompany a lifetime of building businesses—stories they share happily here today.

• • •

LISA, a wife and mother of two, knows well the profound impact of family, and she is deeply grateful to have grown up surrounded by so much love and support. Brought up attending Christian Science Sunday school at Third Church of Christ, Scientist in Dallas, her faith has helped her navigate various challenges throughout her life, including a twelve-year-long loss of hearing.

Being deaf for over a decade facilitated the trajectory of her life. At eighteen years old, Lisa experienced sudden hearing loss at college. She decided to specialize and pursue higher education, receiving her MEd in Deaf Education at Boston University. In Boston, she was welcomed into the Deaf community and immersed in American Sign Language.

After graduating, she taught Deaf children, from those in preschool through high school. After four years of teaching, she went to work at Massachusetts State Association of the Deaf, a non-profit serving and advocating for the Deaf communities, and managing the statewide Family Sign Language Program for families with Deaf and Hard of Hearing children from newborns to three-year-olds. Here she had the opportunity to volunteer with AIDS Action Committee, setting up a Buddy program with Deaf leaders to educate and support their community members impacted by AIDS, as well as participating as a "buddy" herself.

During this period, her family, with their characteristic supportiveness, all worked to learn sign language themselves. Her twin, Laurie, eventually became fluent. Ultimately, Lisa's hearing did return; however, her commitment and connection to the Deaf community has never faltered. Although it may seem counterintuitive to some, Lisa feels the loss of her hearing to be amongst the greatest gifts ever bestowed upon her. Lisa's tenacity and positive outlook are Wyly family traits, and have served her well throughout her lifetime.

Today, with the support of her husband, John, she is working as a certified American Sign Language (ASL) interpreter. Lisa serves on the board of Deaf Action Center, a non-profit that services the Deaf, Hard of Hearing, and Deaf Blind community. She is also active in her church, teaching Sunday school and serving on the board of Third Church of Christ, Scientist. Lisa feels fortunate to live within miles of both her father and Laurie. This physical proximity was particularly beneficial, as much of this book was written in person, the three of them sitting at the very table they grew up having family dinners. The process of crafting this book with her dad and sister granted her deeper insight into her family and their history, and she looks forward to sharing both the business and life lessons she learned in the process of co-authoring her father's story.